Oxford English for
Electrical and Mechanical
Engineering

Eric H. Glendinning

Norman Glendinning,
C Eng, MIMechE

Oxford University Press

Oxford University Press
Great Clarendon Street, Oxford OX2 6DP

Oxford New York
Auckland Bangkok Buenos Aires Cape Town Chennai
Dar es Salaam Delhi Hong Kong Istanbul Karachi
Kolkata Kuala Lumpur Madrid Melbourne
Mexico City Mumbai Nairobi São Paulo Shanghai
Taipei Tokyo Toronto

Oxford and *Oxford English*
are trade marks of Oxford University Press

ISBN 0 19 457392 3

© Oxford University Press 2001

First published 1995
Eighth impression 2003

The publisher and authors of *Oxford English for
Computing*, *Oxford English for Electronics*, and *Oxford
English for Electrical and Mechanical Engineering* would
like to thank the teachers and students of the
following institutions for their advice and assistance
in the preparation of these books:

Italy
Istituti Tecnici Industriali:
  Aldini-Valeriani, Bologna
  Avagado, Turin
  Belluzi, Bologna
  Benedetto Castelli, Brescia
  Conti, Milan
  de Preto, Schio
  Euganeo, Este
  Fermi, Rome
  Fermi, Naples
  Fermi, Vicenza
  Ferrari, Turin
  Gastaldi, Genoa
  Giordani, Naples
  Giorgi, Milan
  Giorgi, Rome
  Hensemberger, Monza
  Leonardo da Vinci, Florence
  Marconi, Verona
  Miano, San Giorgio, Naples
  Paeocapa, Bergamo
  Panetti, Bari
  Pasolini, Milan
  Peano, Turin
  San Felipo Neri, Rome
  Zuccante, Mestre
Istituti Professionali:
  Caselli, Siena
  Cinnici, Florence
  Galileo Galilei, Turin
  Galvani, Milan
Istituto Tecnico Commerciale Lorgna, Verona

France
Ecole Nationale du Commerce, Paris
Lycée Bouchardon, Chaumont
Lycée Monge, Chambery
Lycée du Dauphiné, Romans
Lycée Téchnologique Industriel, Valence

The publisher and authors would like to thank the
following for their kind permission to use articles,
extracts, or adaptations from copyright material.
Every effort has been made to trace the owners of
copyright material in this book, but we should be
pleased to hear from any copyright owner whom we
have been unable to contact in order to rectify any
errors or omissions.

Collins CDT GCSE: Technology by M Horsley and P
Fowler, Collins Educational, an imprint of
HarperCollins Publishers Limited
Eraba Limited, Livingston

The following articles were all taken from *The
Education Guardian*
© *The Guardian*:

'Electric motor' by Helen Davies, 20 April 1993
'Central heating' by J Harker, 8 December 1992
'Fridge' by H Birch, 30 April 1991
'Electronic scales' by H Birch, 10 December 1991
'Wave power' by H Davies, 23 November 1993
'Road breaker' by H Birch, 24 September 1991
'Disk brakes' by R Leedham, 16 March 1993
'Magnetic levitation train' by H Birch, 7 July 1992

'Air Film Material Handling Systems' , Aerofilm
  Systems, The Netherlands.
'Design tools for speed and quality' by John Fox,
  Professional Engineering, June 1993. The adaptation
  of this article is reproduced by permission of the
  Council of the Institution of Mechanical Engineers,
  London, UK.
'Beating the fire risk with water-based hydraulics' by
  P Tweedale, *Professional Engineering*, November
  1993. The adaptation of this article is reproduced
  by permission of the Council of the Institution of
  Mechanical Engineers, London, UK.
'On the make' by Judith Massey, *Personal Computer
  Magazine*, August 1992
'Types of corrosion, how it occurs and what to look
  for', *Design Engineering*, June 1991
Working at a light engineering plant (people at work) by
  T May, Wayland (Publishers) Limited 1982

The publishers would like to thank the following for
permission to reproduce illustrations:

*Computer Shopper; Computervision; The Education
Guardian; Engineering News; Technology Basic Facts* by
C Chapman, M Horsley, and E Small, HarperCollins
Publishers Ltd; Volkswagen UK Ltd

The publishers would like to thank the following for
their permission to reproduce photographs:

British Aerospace; Derek Cattani; DataTech Ltd; The
Engineering Council; The Engineering Training
Authority; Graduates to Industry; Intelligence
Systems; Marconi; Peugeot-Talbot; Lucy Porter;
Rolls-Royce; Salter Houseware; The Science Photo
Library; Scottish Power; Sport for TV; The Telegraph
Colour Library; Volkswagen UK Ltd

Typeset in Monotype Photina and Univers

Printed in China

Technical contents

Contents

1 Engineering – what's it all about?

Tuning-in

Task 1

List the main branches of engineering. Combine your list with others in your group. Then read this text to find out how many of the branches listed are mentioned.

> Engineering is largely a practical activity. It is about putting ideas into action. Civil engineering is concerned with making bridges, roads, airports, etc. Mechanical engineering deals with the design and manufacture of tools and machines. Electrical engineering is about
> 5 the generation and distribution of electricity and its many applications. Electronic engineering is concerned with developing components and equipment for communications, computing, and so on.
>
> Mechanical engineering includes marine, automobile, aeronautical,
> 10 heating and ventilating, and others. Electrical engineering includes electricity generating, electrical installation, lighting, etc. Mining and medical engineering belong partly to mechanical and partly to electrical.

Task 2

Complete the blanks in this diagram using information from the text.

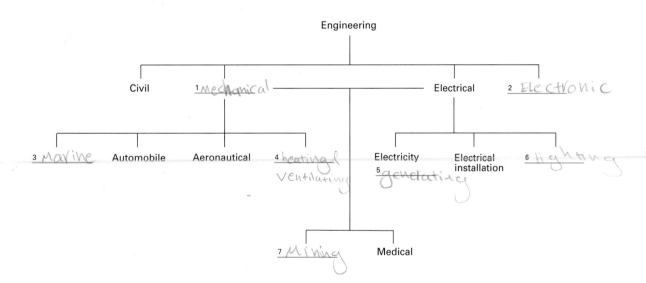

Reading *Introduction*

In your study and work, it is important to think about what you are going to read before you read. This helps you to link old and new knowledge and to make guesses about the meaning of the text. It is also important to have a clear purpose so that you choose the best way to read. In this book, you will find tasks to make you think before you read and tasks to help you to have a clear purpose when you read.

Task 3

Study these illustrations. They show some of the areas in which engineers work. Can you identify them? What kinds of engineers are concerned with these areas – electrical, mechanical, or both?

Food Processing

electrical

mecanical

Medical

CiveL

Task 4

Now read the following texts to check your answers to Task 3. Match each text to one of the illustrations above.

Transport: Cars, trains, ships, and planes are all products of mechanical engineering. Mechanical engineers are also involved in support services such as roads, rail track, harbours, and bridges.

5   Food processing: Mechanical engineers design, develop, and make the machines and the processing equipment for harvesting, preparing and preserving the foods and drinks that fill the supermarkets.

Medical engineering: Body scanners, X-ray machines, life-support systems, and other high-tech equipment result from mechanical and electrical engineers combining with medical experts to convert ideas
10 into life-saving and preserving products.

Building services: Electrical engineers provide all the services we need in our homes and places of work, including lighting, heating, ventilation, air-conditioning, refrigeration, and lifts. *elevetor*

Energy and power: Electrical engineers are concerned with the
15 production and distribution of electricity to homes, offices, industry, hospitals, colleges and schools, and the installation and maintenance of the equipment involved in these processes.

Source: Adapted from *Turning ideas into action*, Institution of Mechanical Engineers, and *Engineering a Career*, Institution of Electronics and Electrical Incorporated Engineers.

Language study *deals with/is concerned with*

What is the link between column **A** and column **B**?

A	**B**
mechanical	machines
electrical	electricity

Column **A** lists a branch of engineering or a type of engineer. Column **B** lists things they are concerned with. We can show the link between them in a number of ways:

1   *Mechanical engineering* **deals with** *machines.*
2   *Mechanical engineers* **deal with** *machines.*
3   *Mechanical engineering* **is concerned with** *machines.*
4   *Mechanical engineers* **are concerned with** *machines.*
5   *Machines* **are the concern of** *mechanical engineers.*

Task 5

Match each item in column **A** with an appropriate item from column **B** and link the two in a sentence.

	A		**B**
1	marine f	**a**	air-conditioning 3
2	aeronautical g	**b**	roads and bridges 6
3	heating and ventilating a	**c**	body scanners 9
4	electricity generating i	**d**	cables and switchgear 8
5	automobile h	**e**	communications and equipment 7
6	civil b	**f**	ships 1
7	electronic e	**g**	planes 2
8	electrical installation d	**h**	cars and trucks 5
9	medical c	**i**	power stations 4

marine deals with ships
"   "   "

Word study *Word stress*

Words are divided into syllables. For example:

engine	en.gine
engineer	en.gin.eer
engineering	en.gin.eer.ing

Each syllable is pronounced separately, but normally only one syllable is stressed. That means it is said more slowly and clearly than the other syllables. We say *'engine* but *engin'eer*. A good dictionary will show the stressed syllables.

Task 6   Listen to these words. Try to mark the stressed syllables.

1   machinery ₂
2   mechanical ₂
3   machine ₂
4   install ₂
5   installation ₃
6   electricity ₃
7   electrical ₂
8   electronics ₃
9   aeronautical ₂
10   ventilation ₃

Writing

Task 7   Fill in the gaps in the following description of the different branches of engineering using information from this diagram and language you have studied in this unit.

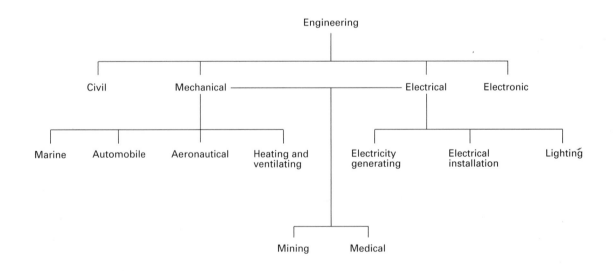

The main branches of engineering are civil, *mechanical*, ²*Electrical*, and electronic. Mechanical engineering is ³*concerned* ⁴*with* machinery of all kinds. This branch of engineering includes ⁵*marine*, automobile, ⁶*Aeronautical* and heating and ventilating. The first three are concerned with transport: ⁷*ships*, cars and planes. The last ⁸*deals* with air-conditioning, refrigeration, etc.

Electrical engineering deals with ⁹*electricity* from generation to use. Electricity generating is concerned with ¹⁰*power* stations. Electrical installation deals ¹¹*with* cables, switchgear, and connecting up electrical equipment.

Two branches of engineering include both ¹²*Mechanical* and ¹³*electrical* engineers. These are mining and ¹⁴*Medical* engineering. The former deals with mines and mining equipment, the latter with hospital ¹⁵*equipment* of all kinds.

the last

Listening

Task 8   Listen to these short extracts. To which branch of engineering do these engineers belong?

Task 9   Listen again. This time note the words which helped you decide on your answers.

2 Choosing a course

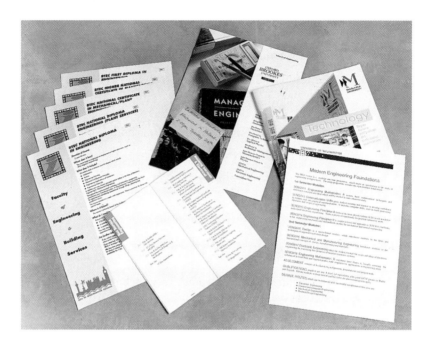

Tuning-in

Task 1

Study this list of points to consider when deciding whether to study engineering. Tick [√] the statements which refer to you. Then ask your partner which statements refer to him or her.

1   You enjoy practical projects – creating and investigating things.

2   You like finding out how things work.

3   You are interested in improving the environment.

4   You like helping people.

5   You enjoy solving problems.

6   You enjoy organizing activities.

7   You enjoy science programmes on TV or on the radio.

8   You sometimes read articles on scientific or engineering topics.

9   You have a lot of determination and stamina.

If you have ticked most of these statements, engineering is the right course of study for you.

Source: Adapted from *Cyberpunks and Technophobes*, BBC Education

Task 2

Fill in the gaps in this text. Each gap represents one word. Compare your answers with your partner. More than one answer is possible for many of the gaps.

In the United Kingdom you can [1]_____ engineering at a college of further education or a university. Most college courses [2]_____ from one to two years. University undergraduate courses [3]_____ engineering last from three to four years.

A college will take [4]_____ after four years of secondary school education. Most students study full-time, [5]_____ day-release courses are available for people who [6]_____ in local engineering companies. Students will be given a certificate [7]_____ a diploma at the [8]_____ of their course.

Most university students will have completed six [9]_____ of secondary school. Others will have taken a diploma course at college. [10]_____ give degrees. A Bachelor's degree [11]_____ three to four years. A Master's [12]_____ requires a further year.

Task 3   📼   Listen to the text and note the words used on the tape for each gap.

Reading *Having a purpose*

As a student of engineering or as a professional engineer, you have to read a great deal. Make a list of some of the kinds of texts you may read. It is important that you develop the most effective skills for getting the information you want quickly and accurately when you read.

Task 4

There are examples on the following pages of some of the kinds of texts you may read in your studies or working life. Match them to this list:

1 table g
2 index e
3 contents a
4 book title b
5 manual f
6 price list of components c
7 college brochure h
8 job advertisement d

title and pages 3

book title

a

Contents

b

Electrical Applications 3

David W. Tyler
C Eng, MIEE

Price list of components

c

6

Order Code	Type	Price each
RK65V	PCB Latch Pl 2w	20p
BX96E	PCB Latch Pl 3w	25p
YW11M	PCB Latch Pl 4w	29p
FY93B	PCB Latch Pl 5w	35p
YW12N	PCB Latch Pl 6w	42p
YW13P	PCB Latch Pl 8w	48p
RK66W	PCB Latch Pl 10w	54p
YW14Q	PCB Latch Pl 12w	58p
BH61R	PCB Latch Pl 17w	60p

index

e

8

generally

job advertisement

d

f

[handwritten: 5 manual]

[handwritten top right: advertisement]

Step	Action
1	Open the top cover
2	Set the MTR switch to MTR mode, that is, move it to the left.
3	Close the top cover
4	Switch the system off
5	Wait 5 seconds

[handwritten: telling to a How to do something]

g

[handwritten: 1 table]

Bearing bore mm	Shaft limits mm	
	Heavy loading	Light loading
-12	—	+0.003 −0.005
12.1–30	—	+0.005 −0.003
30.1–50	—	+0.007 −0.003
50.1–75	+0.018 −0.003	+0.013 −0.000
75.1–100	+0.023 −0.005	+0.016 −0.003
100.1–120	+0.028 −0.010	+0.020 −0.005

h

[handwritten: college brochure 7]

EEB	NATIONAL CERTIFICATE MODULES IN REFRIGERATION (EVENING)

This course provides students with a basic knowledge of the technology of refrigeration, including system elements, procedures and the need for safe working practice.

[handwritten: brochure]

[handwritten: manual]

Task 5   When you read, it is important to have a clear purpose. Here are some of the purposes you may have for reading the above texts. Match one purpose to each text.

1 finding a job
2 pricing a component
3 finding out how to do something
4 choosing the best chapter to read
5 looking for specific information on a topic
6 learning about electrical equipment
7 choosing a course
8 looking for a specification

Task 6

Choosing a course requires careful reading of college and university brochures. Your purpose here is to find the most appropriate course for each of the following prospective students. Use the Course Guide which follows and answer using the course code.

1 A student who has just left school and wants to become a technician.
2 A student who wants to design ships.
3 A student who wants to get an engineering degree and also improve his knowledge of languages.
4 A student who wants a degree eventually but whose qualifications at present are enough to start an HND course.
5 A student who wants to work as an engineer with the air force.
6 A technician employed by a company which installs electrical wiring in factories.
7 A student with a National Certificate in Electrical Engineering who is prepared to spend another two years studying to improve her qualifications.
8 A student interested in how micro-organisms can be used in industry.

Course Guide   **E N G I N E E R I N G**

EE22   Higher National Diploma in Electronic and Electrical Engineering. Two years, full-time. For potential electronic and electrical engineers. The first year is common and the second year allows students to specialize in either electronic or electrical engineering subjects. Successful students may continue to a degree course.

EE17   National Certificate in Electrical Engineering. One year, full-time. For potential technicians or for those who wish to gain entry to an HND course.

EE3   Higher National Certificate Course in Electrical Engineering. Two years, day-release. This course provides the technical education required for senior technicians employed in the electrical installation industry.

H300   Bachelor of Engineering (B Eng) – Mechanical Engineering for Europe. Four years, full-time, including one year study and work attachment in France or Germany.

H400   Bachelor of Engineering (B Eng) – Aeronautical Engineering. Three years, full-time, or four years including one year of professional training in the aircraft industry.

HJ36   Bachelor of Engineering (B Eng) – Naval Architecture and Ocean Engineering. Three years, full-time.

H340   Bachelor of Science (Engineering) – Mechanical

▶

H250 Bachelor of Engineering (B Eng) – Manufacturing Management. A two-year HND course in engineering followed by two years of technology and management designed to produce managers qualified in high technology.

Further information may be obtained by contacting one of these information centres and requesting the appropriate course leaflet by code number.

All **E courses**:

Information Centre
Fraser College
Parlett Street
Glasgow GL2 2KL

All **H courses**:

Information Centre
Maxwell University
Hunter Square
Glasgow GL1 5PN

Writing *Letter writing, 1: requesting information*

Write a letter to either the college or the university mentioned in Task 6 asking for information on a course which interests you. Set out your letter like this:

```
                                        21 Route de St Fargeau
                                               18900 Russe
                                                    FRANCE

                                            30 August 199-

Information Centre
Fraser College
Parlett Street
GLASGOW
GL2 2KL
UK
```

; = more formal

```
Dear Sir/Madam,

Please send me further information on course EE17 -
National Certificate in Electrical Engineering.

Yours faithfully,

Daniel Romero

Daniel Romero
```

3 Engineering materials

[handwritten annotations: skim: take off / skim fat / skim : reading and get an idea]

Ribbed plastic pipes stacked near a road construction site where they will be laid for drainage along the sides of a new section of motorway.

[handwritten annotations: scan phone book / " dictionary. / to scan: to look for specific.]

Tuning-in

Task 1

List the materials you know which are used in engineering. Combine your list with the others in your group and classify the materials as metals, thermoplastics, etc.

Reading *Scanning tables*

In engineering it is important to practise reading tables, charts, diagrams, and graphs because so much information is presented in these ways. We will start in this unit with a table.

Scanning is the best strategy for finding information in a table. With scanning, you know before you read what sort of information you are searching for. To scan a table, you move your eyes up and down the columns until you find the word or words you want. To scan quickly, you must learn to ignore any information which will not help you with your task.

handwritten: malleable: can easily be made into diffrent shape

Task 2

Scan the table which follows to find a material which is:

1. soft *Alu*
2. ductile → *you can bend/change the shape without breaking*
3. malleable *you can do anything you want*
4. tough → *strong*
5. scratch-resistant
6. conductive and malleable *durable: last for long time*
7. durable and hard
8. stiff and brittle
9. ductile and corrosion-resistant
10. heat-resistant and chemical-resistant

handwritten: brittle = hard but easily broken   *tough = you can't destroy easily.*

Materials	Properties	Uses
Metals		
Aluminium *1-2-9*	Light, soft, ductile, highly conductive, corrosion-resistant.	Aircraft, engine components, foil, cooking utensils
Copper *2-3-6-4 9*	Very malleable, tough and ductile, highly conductive, corrosion-resistant.	Electric wiring, PCBs, tubing
Brass (65% copper, 35% zinc)	Very corrosion-resistant. Casts well, easily machined. Can be work hardened. Good conductor.	Valves, taps, castings, ship fittings, electrical contacts
Mild steel (iron with 0.15% to 0.3% carbon) *2-3 -4*	High strength, ductile, tough, fairly malleable. Cannot be hardened and tempered. Low cost. Poor corrosion resistance.	General purpose
High carbon steel (iron with 0.7% to 1.4% carbon)	Hardest of the carbon steels but less ductile and malleable. Can be hardened and tempered.	Cutting tools such as drills, files, saws
Thermoplastics		
ABS *5-4*	High impact strength and toughness, scratch-resistant, light and durable.	Safety helmets, car components, telephones, kitchenware
Acrylic *7*	Stiff, hard, very durable, clear, can be polished easily. Can be formed easily.	Aircraft canopies, baths, double glazing
Nylon *4*	Hard, tough, wear-resistant, self-lubricating.	Bearings, gears, casings for power tools
Thermosetting plastics		
Epoxy resin	High strength when reinforced, good chemical and wear resistance.	Adhesives, encapsulation of electronic components
Polyester resin *10-8*	Stiff, hard, brittle. Good chemical and heat resistance.	Moulding, boat and car bodies
Urea formaldehyde *8-*	Stiff, hard, strong, brittle, heat-resistant, and a good electrical insulator.	Electrical fittings, adhesives

handwritten annotations throughout:
Aluminium (over Properties and Uses columns)
to cast: to put stg in a mold
(for wood) file nail
It doesn't break
stop/cover Canopies of tree
no friction sth stick / sth use for reducing friction / cover
It doesn't get old.

handwritten at bottom: stiff person   corrosion: ...   relationship strat corrosion

23

Task 3 Scan the table to find:

1 A metal used to make aircraft *AL*
2 Plastics used for adhesives *epoxy resion*
3 Steel which can be hardened *hight carbon steel*
4 An alloy suitable for castings *costing*
5 A plastic with very low friction *Nylon*
6 A material suitable for safety helmets *ABS*
7 A metal suitable for a salt-water environment *Brass*
8 A metal for general construction use but which should be protected from corrosion *Mild steel*
9 A plastic for car bodies *poly este resin*
10 The metal used for the conductors in printed circuit boards *Copper*

Language study *Making definitions*

Study these facts from the table about aluminium:

1 Aluminium is a light metal.
2 Aluminium is used to make aircraft.

We can link these facts to make a definition of aluminium:

1+2 *Aluminium is a light metal **which** is used to make aircraft.*

Task 4 Use the table on the previous page to make definitions of each of the materials in column **A**. Choose the correct information in columns **B** and **C** to describe the materials in column **A**.

A	B	C
1 An alloy		allows heat or current to flow easily
2 A thermoplastic		8 remains rigid at high temperatures
3 Mild steel		5 does not allow heat or current to flow easily
4 A conductor	a metal	contains iron and 0.7% to 1.4% carbon
5 An insulator	a material	becomes plastic when heated
6 High carbon steel	an alloy	contains iron and 0.15% to 0.3% carbon
7 Brass		formed by mixing other metals or elements
8 A thermosetting plastic		7 consists of copper and zinc

1 An alloy is a metal which is formed by mixing other------
2 A thermoplastic is a material which becomes --- ---
3 Mild steel is a metal which contans
4 A conductor is a material which allows
5 An insulator is a material which
6 High carbon steel is a metal which contains
7 Brass is an alloy which consists

24

8 A thermosetting plastic is a material which remains

[handwritten top:] nylon which is a self lubricating, hard and tough thermoplastic is used where silent, low friction operation is required such as motorized drives camera

Writing *Adding information to a text*

Study this text about aluminium.

Aluminium is used to make aircraft, engine components, and many items for the kitchen.

We can add extra information to the text like this:

> Aluminium, **which is light, soft, and ductile**, is used to make aircraft, engine components – **for example, cylinder heads** – and many items for the kitchen, **such as pots**.

Note that the extra information is marked with commas or dashes:

, which ... ,
– for example, ... –
, such as ... ,

[handwritten:] Acrylic which is a hard, durable and clear thermo plastic can be formed in several ways, and has many uses, such as aircraft canopies and double glazing.

Task 5

Add this extra information to the following text about plastics.

1   Plastics can be moulded into plates, car components, and medical aids.
2   Thermoplastics soften when heated again and again.
3   Thermosetting plastics set hard and do not alter if heated again.
4   ABS is used for safety helmets.
5   Nylon is self-lubricating.
6   Nylon is used for motorized drives in cameras.
7   Acrylic is a clear thermoplastic.
8   Acrylic is used for aircraft canopies and double glazing.
9   Polyester resin is used for boat and car bodies.
10 Polyester resin is hard and has good chemical and heat resistance.

[handwritten:] Polyester resin which is a thermosetting plastic used for casting such as boats and car bodies has a number useful properties for example it's hard and has a good chemical and heat resistance

Plastics are synthetic materials. They can be softened and moulded into useful articles. They have many applications in engineering. There are two types of plastics: thermoplastics and thermosetting plastics.

ABS is a thermoplastic which is tough and durable. Because it has high impact strength, it has applications where sudden loads may occur.

Nylon is a hard, tough thermoplastic. It is used where silent, low-friction operation is required.

Acrylic can be formed in several ways. It is hard, durable, and has many uses.

Polyester resin is a thermosetting plastic used for castings. It has a number of useful properties.

[handwritten:] 1 plastics which are synthetic material can be moulded and softened into useful articels such as plates, car components and medical aids They have many applications in engineering. There are two types of plastics thermoplastics which soften when heated again and again and thermosetting plastics which set hard and do not alter if heated again. ABS is a thermoplastic which is tough durable and is used for safety helmets because it has high impact strength it has applications where sudden loads may occur

4 Mechanisms

the way s.th is work
method or procedure for doing stg.

Tuning-in

Task 1

Identify these simple mechanisms. Try to explain the principles on which they operate.

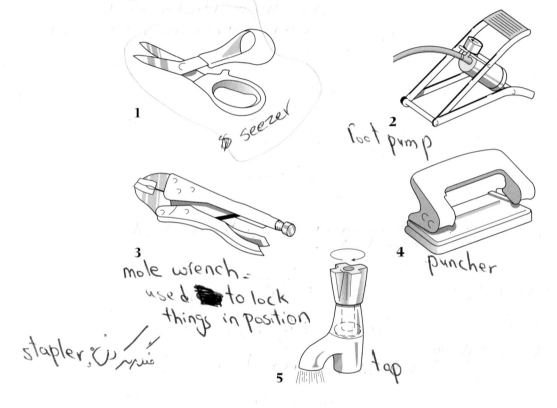

1 *seezer*

2 *foot pump*

3 *mole wrench = used to lock things in position*

stapler, دبّاسة / مشبك

4 *puncher*

5 *tap*

Reading *Scanning a text*

Scanning is the best strategy for searching for specific information in a text. Move your eyes up and down the text until you find the word or words you want. Again, try to ignore any information which will not help you with your task.

Task 2

Scan the text opposite quickly to find out which of these mechanisms are mentioned.

1   cam *20*
2   tap *2*
3   pendulum *13*

4   foot pump
5   escalator *3*

Mechanisms

Mechanisms are an important part of everyday life. They allow us to do simple things like switch on lights, turn taps, and open doors. They also make it possible to use escalators and lifts, travel in cars, and fly from continent to continent.

5 Mechanisms play a vital role in industry. While many industrial processes have electronic control systems, it is still mechanisms that deliver the power to do the work. They provide the forces to press steel sheets into car body panels, to lift large components from place to place, to force plastic through dies to make pipes.

10 All mechanisms involve some kind of motion. The four basic kinds of motion are:

Rotary: Wheels, gears, and rollers involve rotary movement.

Oscillating: The pendulum of a clock oscillates – it swings backwards and forwards.

15 Linear: The linear movement of a paper trimmer is used to cut the edge of the paper.

Reciprocating: The piston in a combustion engine reciprocates.

Many mechanisms involve changing one kind of motion into another type. For example, the reciprocating motion of a piston is changed 20 into a rotary motion by the crankshaft, while a cam converts the rotary motion of the engine into the reciprocating motion required to operate the valves.

Task 3   Now read the text to find the answers to these questions.

1   What does a cam do?
2   What does oscillating mean?
3   How are plastic pipes formed?
4   What simple mechanisms in the home are mentioned directly or indirectly?
5   What is the function of a crankshaft?
6   Give an example of a device which can produce a linear movement.
7   How are car body panels formed?
8   What do mechanisms provide in industry?

Writing   *Ways of linking ideas, 1*

When we write, we may have to describe, explain, argue, persuade, complain, etc. In all these forms of writing, we use ideas. To make our writing effective, we have to make sure our readers can follow our ideas. One way of helping our readers is to make the links between the ideas in our writing.

What are the links between these pairs of ideas? What words can we use to mark the links?

1   Mechanisms are important to us.
2   They allow us to travel.

3   Mechanisms deliver the power to do work.
4   They play a vital role in industry.

5   Friction is sometimes a help.
6   It is often a hindrance.

27

Sentence 2 is a *reason* for sentence 1. We can link 1 and 2 like this:

Mechanisms are important to us **because/since/as** *they allow us to travel.*

Sentence 4 is the *result* of sentence 3. We can link 3 and 4 like this:

Mechanisms deliver the power to do work **so** *they play a vital role in industry.*
        Mechanisms deliver the power to do work; **therefore** *they play a vital role in industry.*

Sentence 6 *contrasts* with sentence 5. We can link 5 and 6 like this:

Friction is sometimes a help **but** *it is often a hindrance.*

Task 4

Show the links between these sets of ideas using appropriate linking words.

1 Copper is highly conductive. so
    It is used for electric wiring.
2 Weight is measured in newtons. but
    Mass is measured in kilograms.
3 Nylon is used for bearings. because
    It is self-lubricating.
4 ABS has high impact strength. Because so
    It is used for safety helmets.
5 The foot pump is a class 2 lever.
    The load is between the effort and the fulcrum. because
6 Friction is essential in brakes.
  it Friction is a nuisance in an engine. but

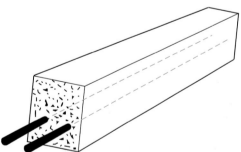

Compression

Neutral axis

Tension

Load

7 The upper surface of a beam is in compression. but but
    The lower surface is in tension.

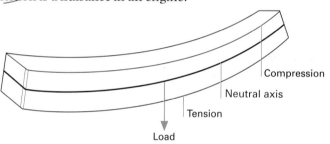

8 Concrete beams have steel rods near the lower surface.
because Concrete is weak in tension.
    it

Language study *Dealing with technical terms*

One of the difficult things about the English of engineering is that there are many technical terms to learn. Newer terms may be the same, or almost the same, in your own language. But many terms will be quite different and you may not always remember them.

When this happens, you will have to use whatever English you know to make your meaning clear.

The same thing may happen in reverse when you know a technical term but the person you are communicating with does not recognize it. This may happen in the *Speaking practice* tasks in this book. Again, when this happens, you will have to make your meaning clear using other words.

Task 5

The technical words in column **A** are similar in meaning to the more general English in column **B**. Match them.

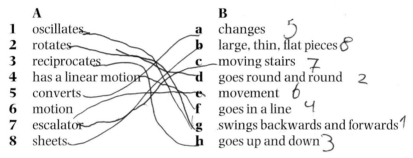

	A		B
1	oscillates	a	changes
2	rotates	b	large, thin, flat pieces
3	reciprocates	c	moving stairs
4	has a linear motion	d	goes round and round
5	converts	e	movement
6	motion	f	goes in a line
7	escalator	g	swings backwards and forwards
8	sheets	h	goes up and down

Task 6

Try to explain how this simple mechanism operates using whatever English you know. Write your explanation down. Compare your explanation with the technical explanation given on page 4 of the Answer Book. Learn any technical terms which are unfamiliar to you.

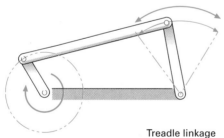

Treadle linkage

Speaking practice

Task 7

Work in pairs, **A** and **B**. Each of you has a diagram of a cam. Describe your diagram to your partner. Your partner should try to reproduce your diagram from the spoken description you provide.

Student A: Your diagram is on page 177.
Student B: Your diagram is on page 181.

Thes text on the next page will help you with the vocabulary you need.

Cams are shaped pieces of metal or plastic fixed to, or part of, a
rotating shaft. A 'follower' is held against the cam, either by its own
weight or by a spring. As the cam rotates, the follower moves. The
way in which it moves and the distance it moves depends on the
5 shape of the cam. Rotary cams are the most common type. They are
used to change rotary motion into either reciprocating or oscillating
motion.

If you do not understand what your partner says, these questions and phrases
may be helpful.

1 Could you say that again/repeat that, please?
2 What do you mean by X?
3 Where exactly is the X?
4 What shape is the X?
5 How does the X move?

If your partner does not understand you, try to rephrase what you say.

unit 5

4 – Forces

buoyancy = ability that stg has to float on a liquid or in the air
elasticity = ability of a material to return to its original shape, size
and condition after it has been stretched.
friction = force which prevents things from falling or sliding.
gravity = force which causes things to drop to the ground

[handwritten: Force= stg that pushes or pulls and creates movement]

5 Forces in engineering

[handwritten: Forces {Friction, buoyancy=ability that stg has to float on a liquid or in the air, elasticity=ability of a material to its, gravity}]

Tuning-in

Task 1

Working in your group, try to explain these problems.

1. Why doesn't the ship sink?
2. What makes the spring stretch and what keeps the weight up?
3. Why doesn't the box slide down the slope? _[handwritten: friction]_

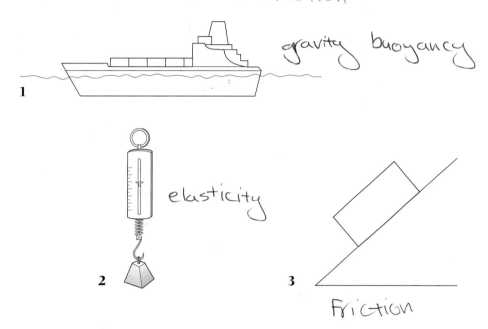

[handwritten labels: 1 — gravity buoyancy; 2 — elasticity; 3 — friction]

Reading 1 _Predicting_

As you learnt in Unit 1, it is important to think about what you are going to read before you read. Do not start to read a text immediately. One way to help your reading is to think about the words which might appear in the text. The title might help to focus your thoughts. Which words might appear in a text with the title _Forces in engineering_?

Task 2

The text you are going to read is called _Forces in engineering_. Here are some of the words it contains. Can you explain the link between each word and the title of the text?

weight	buoyancy	equilibrium
elasticity	magnitude _[handwritten: size and]_	resultant _[handwritten: = single of a number of different forces of vectors]_
newton	gravity	

exert = to force or pressure in a strong determined
to calibrate = to adjust sth so that it can be used to meas
sth accura

Task 3

Now read the text. Use the information in the text to check the explanations you made in Task 1.

Forces in engineering

To solve the ship problem, we must look at the forces on the ship (Fig. 1). The weight, W, acts downwards. That is the gravity force. The buoyancy force, B, acts upwards. Since the ship is in equilibrium, the resultant force is zero, so the magnitudes of B and W must be the

5 same.

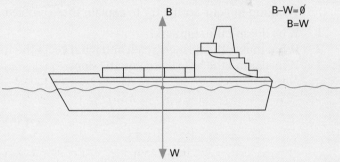

$$B - W = \emptyset$$
$$B = W$$

Fig. 1

Another very important force in engineering is the one caused by elasticity. A good example of this is a spring. Springs exert more force the more they are stretched. This property provides a way of measuring force. A spring balance can be calibrated in newtons, the

10 unit of force. The block in Fig. 2 has a weight of 10 newtons. The weight on the balance pulls the spring down. To give equilibrium, the spring pulls up to oppose that weight. This upward force, F1, equals the weight of the block, W.

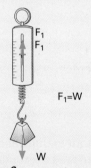

$$F_1 = W$$

Fig. 2

It is important to get the distinction between mass and weight

15 absolutely clear. Mass is the quantity of matter in an object. Weight is the force on that object due to gravity. Mass is measured in kilograms, whereas weight, being a force, is measured in newtons.

We have looked at buoyancy, elasticity, and gravity. There is a fourth force important in engineering, and that is friction. Friction is a help in

20 some circumstances but a hindrance in others. Let us examine the forces on the box (Fig. 3). Firstly, there is its weight, W, the gravity force, then there is the reaction, R, normal to the plane. R and W have a resultant force trying to pull the box down the slope. It is the friction force, F, acting up the slope, that stops it sliding down.

hindrance = obstacle

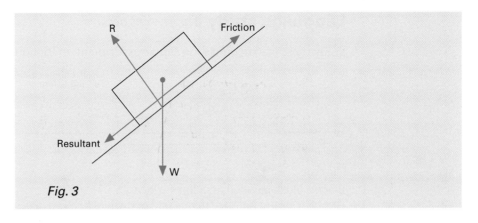

Fig. 3

Reading 2 *Grammar links in texts*

One of the ways in which sentences in a text are held together is by grammar links. In this extract, note how each expression in italics links with an earlier expression.

> Another very important force in engineering is *the one* caused by elasticity. A good example of *this* is a spring. Springs exert more force the more *they* are stretched. *This* property provides a way of measuring force.

Sometimes these links cause problems for readers because they cannot make the right connection between words in different parts of a text.

Study these common grammar links:

1 A repeated noun becomes a pronoun.
   Springs becomes *they.*

2 A word replaces an earlier expression.
   Force in engineering becomes *one.*

3 A word replaces a whole sentence or clause.
   Springs exert more force the more they are stretched becomes *This property.*

Task 4

With which earlier expressions do the words in italics link? Join them as in the example above.

> Friction in machines is destructuve and wasteful. *It* causes the moving parts to wear and *it* produces heat where *it* is not wanted. Engineers reduce friction by using very highly polished materials and by lubricating *their* surfaces with oil and grease. *They* also use ball
> 5 bearings and roller bearings because rolling objects cause less friction than sliding *ones.*

Source: S. Larkin and L. Bernbaum (eds.), The Penguin Book of the Physical World

Language study *The present passive*

Study these instructions for a simple experiment on friction.

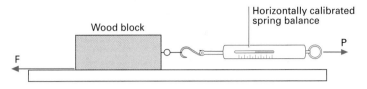

Fig. 4

1 Place a block of wood on a flat surface. ~~is placed~~
2 Attach a spring balance to one end of the block. ~~is attached~~
3 Apply a gradually increasing force to the balance.
④ Note the force at which the block just begins to move. ~~is noted~~
5 Pull the block along so that it moves at a steady speed.
6 Note the force required to maintain movement. *is noted*
7 Compare the two forces. ~~are compared~~

When we describe this experiment, we write:

> A block of wood *is placed* on a flat surface. A spring balance *is attached* to one end of the block.

This description uses the present passive. We form the present passive using *is/are* + past participle.

Task 5

Complete this description of the experiment using the present passive.

A block of wood [1] ~~is placed~~ on a flat surface. A spring balance [2] ~~is attached~~ to one end of the block. A gradually increasing force [3] ~~is applied~~ to the balance. The force at which the block just begins to move [4] ~~is noted~~.

The block [5] ~~is pulled~~ along at a steady speed. The force required to maintain movement [6] ~~is noted~~. The two forces [7] ~~are compared~~. It is found that the first force is greater than the second.

What does this experiment show?

Listening *Listening to lectures*

The listening passage you are going to hear is an extract from a typical engineering lecture. Here are some of the features of lectures.

1 Incomplete sentences: Spoken language is not divided neatly into sentences and paragraphs. For example:
Now what I thought I might do today ... What we are going to talk of ...

2 Repetition and rephrasing: Lecturers often say the same thing more than once and in more than one way. For example:
It will turn, revolve.

3 Signpost expressions: Lecturers often use expressions to help the students know what they are going to do next, what is important, etc. For example:
What we are going to talk of is the extension of a force.

In the same way as when reading, it is helpful to think about the topic of a lecture before you listen. The topic here is *The Moment of a Force*. Can you explain the links between these words from the lecture and the topic? Use a dictionary to help you if necessary.

turning	distance	product
pivot	perpendicular	leverage
fulcrum	hinge	

Task 7

Now listen to the lecture to check your explanations.

Task 8

During the lecture, the lecturer drew this diagram on the board. Which of the words in Task 6 can be used to talk about the diagram?

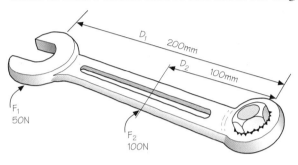

Task 9

Here are some signpost expressions from the lecture. What do you think the lecturer is indicating each time? Select from the labels below, **a** to **e**.

1 We're going to talk about the moment of a force. d
2 If you can think of a spanner e.
3 But what you have to remember is a
4 Something simple to illustrate. e
5 I'm thinking of a practical job. e
6 Why do we put a handle there on the door? e
7 Is that understood? All right? c
8 Well that is then a little explanation of how you calculate moments. b

a Emphasizing an important point
b Showing that the lecture is over
c Checking that the students can follow him
d Introducing the topic of the lecture
e Giving examples to illustrate the points

Task 10

Listen to the tape again and answer these questions according to the information given by the lecturer.

1 What advantage does a longer spanner offer in loosening a tight nut?
2 What is the formula for calculating the moment of a force?
3 Why is it sometimes difficult to apply a force at right angles in a motor car engine?
4 Why is the handle of a door at the edge?
5 Write down the formulae for calculating force and distance.

6 The electric motor

Tuning-in

Task 1

Working in your group, list as many items as you can in the home which use electric motors. Which room has the most items?

Reading *Skimming*

In Unit 3 you studied scanning – locating specific information quickly. Another useful strategy is reading a text quickly to get a general idea of the kind of information it contains. You can then decide which parts of the text are worth reading in more detail later, depending on your reading purpose. This strategy is called *skimming*.

Task 2

Skim this text and identify the paragraphs which contain information on each of these topics. The first one has been done for you.

a What electric motors are used for   *paragraph 1*

b The commutator   6

c Why the armature turns   5

d Electromagnets   2

e Effect of putting magnets together   4 3

f The armature   4 4

---

para

In an electric motor an electric current and magnetic field produce   1
a turning movement. This can drive all sorts of machines, from
wrist-watches to trains. The motor shown in Fig. 1 is for a washing
machine. It is a universal motor, which can run on direct current or
5 alternating current.

An electric current running through a wire produces a magnetic   2
field around the wire. If an electric current flows around a loop of
wire with a bar of iron through it, the iron becomes magnetized. It is
called an electromagnet; one end becomes a north pole and the
10 other a south pole, depending on which way the current is flowing
around the loop.

▶

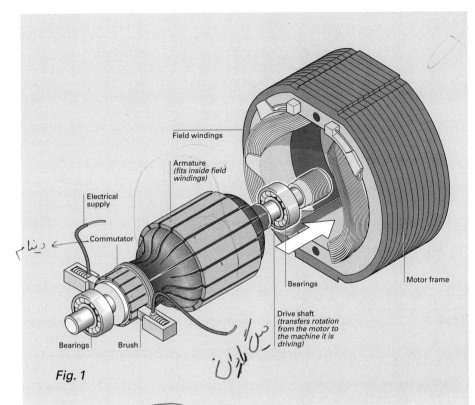

Field windings

Armature
(fits inside field
windings)

Electrical
supply

Commutator

Bearings

Motor frame

Bearings

Drive shaft
(transfers rotation
from the motor to
the machine it is
driving)

Brush

Fig. 1

If you put two magnets close together, like poles – for example, two north poles – repel each other, and unlike poles attract each other.

3

15 In a simple electric motor, like the one shown in Fig. 2, a piece of iron with loops of wire round it, called an armature, is placed between the north and south poles of a stationary magnet, known as the field magnet. When electricity flows around the armature wire, the iron becomes an electromagnet.

4

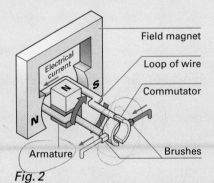

Field magnet

Electrical
current

Loop of wire

Commutator

N S

N

Armature

Brushes

Fig. 2

▶

20 The attraction and repulsion between the poles of this armature   5
magnet and the poles of the field magnet make the armature turn.
As a result, its north pole is close to the south pole of the field
magnet. Then the current is reversed so the north pole of the
armature magnet becomes the south pole. Once again, the
25 attraction and repulsion between it and the field magnet make it
turn. The armature continues turning as long as the direction of the
current, and therefore its magnetic poles, keeps being reversed.

To reverse the direction of the current, the ends of the armature   6
wire are connected to different halves of a split ring called a
30 commutator. Current flows to and from the commutator through
small carbon blocks called brushes. As the armature turns, first one
half of the commutator comes into contact with the brush
delivering the current, and then the other, so the direction of the
current keeps being reversed.

Source: Adapted from 'Inside out: Electric Motor', *Education Guardian*

Task 3

Match each of these diagrams with the correct description, **A**, **B**, **C**, or **D**. One
of the descriptions does *not* match any of the diagrams. (The diagrams are in
the correct sequence, but the descriptions are not.)

Motor run on direct current

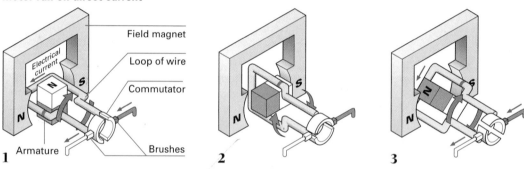

A

The armature turns a quarter of a turn. Then electric contact is broken because
of the gap in the commutator, but the armature keeps turning because there is
nothing to stop it.

B

When current flows, the armature becomes an electromagnet. Its north pole is
attracted by the south pole and repelled by the north pole of the field magnet.

C

When a universal motor is run on direct current, the magnetic poles in the
armature change while those of the field magnet remain constant.

D

When the commutator comes back into contact with the brushes, current
flows through the armature in the opposite direction. Its poles are reversed and
the turn continues.

Language study *Describing function*

en ʒa
① subj + verb + obj

Try to answer this question:

an
② The function of + noun is t + infinitive *to ʔues*

What does an electric motor do?

When we answer a question like this, we describe the function of something.
We can describe the function of an electric motor in this way:

An electric motor converts electrical energy to mechanical energy. α
an noun *verb* *obj*
We can emphasize the function like this:

The function of an electric motor is to convert electrical energy to mechanical α
energy. *noun, is to ʔuse*

③ Passive voice: An electric motor is used to these form, for + ing
to be used, to, for

Task 4
Match each of these motor components to its function, and then describe its
function in a sentence.

Component		Function	
1	armature	a	transfers rotation from the motor
2	bearings	b	create an electromagnetic field
3	brushes	c	converts electromagnetic energy to rotation
4	commutator	d	reverses the current to the armature
5	drive shaft	e	support the drive shaft
6	field windings	f	supply current to the armature

the armature converts . . .

Writing *Describing components*

Task 5
Dismantle this simple dc motor into its components by completing the
labelling of the chart below.

to take sth apart

DC motor

*Dismantle ≠ assemble
(to put stg together)*

to dismantle sth into

direct current

1 *Field magnet*
2 *Armature*
3 *Commutator*   Loop of wire
4 *brushes*

Now study this description of the motor.

A simple dc motor *consists of* a field magnet and an armature. The armature *is placed between* the poles of the magnet. The armature *is made up of* a loop of wire and a split ring *known as* a commutator. The loop *is connected to* the commutator. Current is supplied to the motor through carbon blocks *called* brushes.

To write a description, you need to use language to:

1   dismantle a piece of equipment into its main parts. These expressions will help:

consists of → active verb

A A   *is made up of*   X and Y

is composed of   X ... Y   passive verb

2   name components:

Carbon blocks   *known as* / *called*   brushes.   are known as / are called

3   locate components:

The armature *is placed between* the poles.

4   connect components:

The loop *is connected to* the commutator.

Task 6   Complete the text with the help of the diagram on the next page. Use the following words:

are made up
is placed
is composed
consists

is made up of

A transformer _____ of two coils, a primary and a secondary. The coils are wound on a former which is mounted on a core. The coils *consist* _____ of a number of loops of wire. The core *is composed* _____ of thin pieces of soft iron. U- and T-shaped pieces are used. The former *is placed* _____ on the leg of the T.

Now label the diagram opposite using the completed text.

coil: ملفوف

wind   wound   wound

mounted = attach/fix ثبّت

to mount sth on sth else = to attach one thing firmly to another large thing that supports it

bonded: bond with people
(special connection with tha...)

adhesive = a substance used to make 2 things stick together.

to bond: to connect with adhesive

1 Transformer

2 Coil

3 Core

4 former

5 loops of wire

6 T shape piece of iron

7 U shape piece of iron

Word study

Study these expressions for describing how components are connected to each other.

A is bolted to B. = A is connected to B with bolts.
A is welded to B. = A is connected to B by welding.
A is fixed to B. = no specific method given.

Task 7

Explain each of these methods of connection.

1 screwed *screw*
2 soldered *(use third metal to connect two metal). ing*
3 attached
4 wired *wires*
5 bonded
6 glued *glue*
7 riveted *rivetes*
8 welded *welding*
9 brazed *(Connected using brass or zinc)*
10 nailed *nails*

a bolt: a screw with a flat top and no point to fasten 2 pieces of metal together.

a solder: to fasten or repair metal surface by using solder, which is a soft metal, usually a mixture of lead and tin (which can be melted).

7 An engineering student

Tuning-in

Task 1

List some of the subjects studied by engineering students. Share your list with others in your group.

Task 2

Find out what these terms mean in education. Use a dictionary if necessary.

1 pass
2 resit
3 assessment
4 fail
5 drop out
6 period
7 full-time
8 module

Listening

When listening, it is important to have a clear purpose so that you can concentrate on the parts of the message which best meet your needs. It also helps to think about what you will hear before you listen. The next two tasks will help you to prepare for listening and to have a clear purpose.

Task 3

You are going to hear an interview with David, a student of electrical engineering at a Scottish college of further education. He is a mature student with previous service in the Navy.

Here is David's weekly timetable. Some of the information is missing. Before you listen, try to answer these questions about the timetable.

1 What time does David start each day?
2 When does he finish?
3 How long is a class?
4 How many classes does he have each week?
5 What do the numbers mean after each class, e.g. 150?
6 How often does he have breaks?

	MONDAY	TUESDAY	WEDNESDAY	THURSDAY	FRIDAY
8.45-10.15	Design and make 150	_____ 053	_____ 063	Technology 138	Technology 051
	a. m. b r e a k				
10.30–12.00	Design and make 150	_____ 140	Tutorial 063	_____ 406	_____ 051
	L U N C H B R E A K				
13.00–14.30	_____ 510	Maths 510	Communications 606	_____ 510	Maths 510
	p. m. b r e a k				
14.45–16.15	Technology 053	Principles 138	Technology 038	Principles 051	Self-study

Task 4

Listen to Parts 1 and 2 of the interview in turn. Answer these questions. Compare your answers with a partner.

Part 1

1 What is the name of David's course?
2 How long is the course?
3 How old is David?
4 How long was he in the Navy?
5 How many types of submarines are there?

Part 2

6 How many weeks of teaching does he have left?
7 How is the course assessed?
8 What happens if you fail the tests once?
9 How many are in his class?
10 What kind of problems has he had?

Task 5   🖻   Listen to Part 3 of the interview. Try to complete the information missing from the timetable. Compare your answers with a partner.

Task 6   🖻   Listen to the last part of the interview. Answer these questions.

Part 4

11 When does he practise sport?
12 Where can you go for sport?
13 What kind of sports can you practise there?
14 What is he going to do after the Certificate?
15 What does he want to be?

Task 7   🖻   Now listen to the whole tape. Answer these more difficult questions.

1 Why did David leave the Navy?
2 Why did students drop out of the class?
3 Why did he dislike school?
4 Why do most students find PSD a bit of a nuisance?
5 Why does he want to know when it's raining?
6 Why does he not have to use the library?
7 Why does he enjoy technology most?

Writing *Comparing and contrasting*

Task 8   Write your own timetable in English.

MONDAY	TUESDAY	WEDNESDAY	THURSDAY	FRIDAY

Task 9   Now complete this table. Note any similarities and differences between David's week and your own.

David's subjects	Hours per week	Your subjects	Hours per week

Task 10   Write a short comparison and contrast of your timetable and David's. These expressions may be useful:

more time/hours/classes/maths than
less time/maths/physics than
fewer hours/classes than
not as much time/maths/physics as
not as many hours/classes as
start/finish earlier/later than

Note that *less* and *much* are used for things which cannot be counted.

[handwritten at top: to=ignite =turn sth on through flame]
[handwritten: water heater=boiler]

8 Central heating

[handwritten: Pilot light=it ignite tho boiler]

Tuning-in

Task 1

How can you heat a house in cold weather? List the possible ways.

Reading *Predicting*

In Unit 5 we learnt how using the title can help us to predict the contents of a text. Diagrams are also very useful in helping the reader to make the right guesses about what a text will contain. Before you read a text, read the title and look at any diagrams it contains.

Task 2

Using the diagram, try to explain the function of these components:

1 the pilot light
2 the heat exchanger fins
3 the flue *[handwritten: it allowods air and gases to escape.]*
4 the thermostat
5 the pump

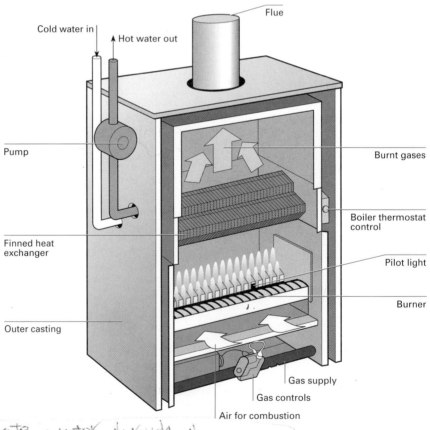

Flue

Cold water in

Hot water out

Pump

Burnt gases

Finned heat exchanger

Boiler thermostat control

Pilot light

Burner

Outer casting

Gas supply

Gas controls

Air for combustion

[handwritten: Circulate water through the system]

feed = tube which supplies a machine with fuel

Task 3

Scan this text quickly to check the explanations you made in Task 2. You may not find all the information you want.

Gas central heating

Most gas central heating works on the 'wet' system of heat transfer between water flowing through pipes. A typical system includes a boiler, a network of pipes, a feed, an expansion tank, radiators, and a hot water storage system.

5 In conventional boilers, water is heated by gas burners. It is then pumped around the central heating system and the hot water storage cylinder. The flow of gas to the burner is controlled by a valve (or valves) which can be operated by a time switch or by a boiler thermostat, hot water cylinder thermostat, or by a
10 thermostat located in one of the rooms.

Air is necessary for complete combustion and is supplied to the burners either from inside the house, when adequate ventilation must be ensured, or directly from outside through a balanced flue.

Water is circulated through a heat exchanger above the burner. The
15 heat exchanger is made of tubes of cast iron or copper, which resist corrosion. Both types use fins to increase the surface area in contact with water, which improves the transfer of heat. A thermostat located in the boiler causes the gas control valve to shut off when the water temperature reaches the pre-set level.

20 After being pumped through a diverter or priority valve, water circulates around either one of two loops of pipework, which act as heat exchangers. One loop passes through the inside of the hot water storage cylinder in a coil arrangement. Heat is transferred to the surrounding water, which can then be drawn off from this
25 cylinder from various hot taps in the house when required. The loop then returns to the boiler for re-heating.

The other loop of the circuit passes to the radiators, which provide room heating. Several radiators are generally connected, where one pipe provides the hot water input and the other carries the cold
30 water back to the boiler. In this way, all radiators receive hot water directly from the boiler.

Source: 'Inside out: Central Heating', *Education Guardian*

Task 4

Put these statements in the correct sequence. The first and last have been done for you.

1	**a**	Water is circulated through a heat exchanger.	1
5	**b**	The loop returns to the boiler for re-heating.	5
4	**c**	One loop passes through the inside of the hot water storage cylinder in a coil of pipes.	4
2	**d**	Water is heated by gas burners.	2
3	**e**	The hot water is pumped through a diverter valve.	3
6	**f**	The other loop of the circuit passes to the radiators.	6
7	**g**	Cold water from the radiators returns to the boiler.	7

Task 5

Use the statements in Task 4 to label the stages shown in this diagram of a heating system.

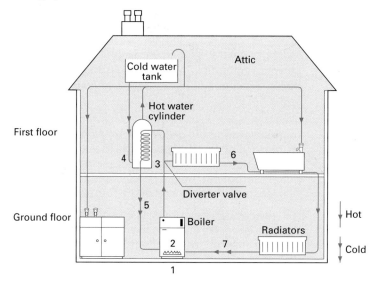

Language study *Time clauses*

What is the relationship between these pairs of actions? How can we link each pair to show this relationship?

1 Cold water passes through a heat exchanger.
  The water is heated.
2 The water is heated.
  It reaches a pre-set temperature.
3 The water is heated.
  It is pumped to a diverter valve.
4 The water temperature reaches the right level.
  The gas control valve shuts off.

We can show how actions are linked in time by using time clauses.

We can use *as* to link two connected actions happening at the same time. For example:

  1 *As cold water passes through a heat exchanger, the water is heated.*

We can use *until* to link an action and the limit of that action. For example:

  2 *The water is heated **until** it reaches a pre-set temperature.*

Note that *until* normally comes between the stages.

We can use *after* to show that one action is followed by another action. For example:

  3 ***After** the water is heated, it is pumped to a diverter valve.*

We can use *when* to show that one action happens immediately after another. For example:

  4 ***When** the water temperature reaches the right level, the gas control valve shuts off.*

Note that when the time word comes first in the sentence, a comma (,) is used after the time clause.

Task 6   Link these sets of actions with appropriate time words.

1   The system is switched on.
    Cold water passes through a heat exchanger in the boiler.

2   The water passes through the heat exchanger.
    The water becomes hotter and hotter.
    The water reaches a pre-set level.

3   The water temperature reaches the pre-set level.
    A thermostat causes the gas control valve to shut off.

4   The water is pumped to a diverter valve.
    The water goes to the hot water cylinder or the radiators.

5   Hot water passes through the inside of the hot water storage cylinder in a coil arrangement.
    Heat is transferred to the surrounding water.

6   The hot water flows through the radiators.
    The hot water loses heat.

7   The water passes through the radiators.
    The water returns to the boiler.

Word study

Task 7   The words listed in the first column of this table are common in descriptions of technical plant. They describe how substances are moved from one stage of the process to the next. Some of these words can be used for any substance; others are more specific. Write an X under Solids, Liquids, or Gases if the word on the left can be used to talk about them. The first example has been done for you.

	Solids	Liquids	Gases
carried	X	X	X
circulated			
conveyed			
distributed			
fed			
piped			
pumped			
supplied			

9 Safety at work

Tuning-in

Task 1

What do these warning labels on chemicals mean? Match each label to the correct warning.

a Highly flammable cause flame
harmless ≠ b Harmful
c Explosive
d Corrosive
e Oxidizing
f Toxic

**MAKE SURE YOU LEARN THE LABELS!
THEY ARE FOR YOUR PROTECTION.**

Toxic   Corrosive   highly flammable   explosive

1 = f   2 = d   3 = a   4 = c

harmful   oxidizing

5 = b   6 = e

Task 2   List some of the potential dangers in your laboratory, workshop, or place of work. How is the risk of these hazards reduced?

Task 3   Study the safety instructions from a workshop below, and then answer these questions.

a   Who are the instructions for?
b   Who wrote them?
c   What was the writer's purpose?

لباس اپنی پرستقان

1   Wear protective clothing at all times.

2   Always wear eye protection when operating lathes, cutters, and grinders and ensure the guard is in place.   براہ

3   Keep your workplace tidy.   شیتھ

4   The areas between benches and around machines must be kept clear.

5   Tools should be put away when not in use and any breakages and losses reported.

6   Machines should be cleaned after use.

Reading   *Understanding the writer's purpose*

Knowing what the writer's purpose is, who the writer is, and who the intended readers are can help us to understand a text. The safety instructions in Task 3 are clearly intended to encourage employees to be safety conscious and reduce the risk of accidents. The writer is perhaps a supervisor or the company safety officer, and the intended readers are machine operatives. Knowing these things can help us to work out the meaning of any part of the text we may not understand.

Task 4   Study the company document on safety on the next page, and then answer these questions.

1   Who is this document for?
   a   machine operatives
   b   managers
   c   all employees
   d   injured employees

2   Who wrote this document?
   a   trade union representative
   b   technician
   c   manager
   d   medical staff

3   What is the writer's intention?
   a   to prevent accidents
   b   to ensure speedy help for injured employees
   c   to protect the company
   d   to warn about dangers

Accident investigation

Whenever an accident occurs that results in an injury (medical case), damage of equipment and material, or both, prompt accident investigation by the immediate manager is required. A written preliminary investigation will be completed by the end of the particular shift or business day on which the accident occurred.

In no event should there be a delay of more than 24 hours. Failure to comply with this requirement may subject the immediate manager to disciplinary action up to and including discharge.

Without adequate accident investigation data the Company may be subjected to costs, claims, and legal action for which it has no defence.

As a minimum, the preliminary accident investigation report will include the following:

1 Name, occupation, and sex of injured worker.
2 Place and date / time of accident.
3 Description of how the accident happened.
4 Immediate causes of the accident – unsafe acts and unsafe conditions.
5 Contributing causes – manager safety performance, level of worker training, inadequate job procedure, poor protective maintenance, etc.
6 Witness(es) – name and department.
7 Corrective action taken – when.

The employee who was injured and any employee(s) who witnessed the incident should be separately interviewed as soon as possible. A copy of the report must be submitted to the Manager – Human Resources for review. Another copy of the report is to be retained for a period of not less than the injured employee's length of employment plus five (5) years.

Task 5

Study this brief report of an accident. In which points does it not meet company policy on reporting accidents?

To:	Name	Department & Location	Date
	Manager	Human Resources	17 May
From:	Name	Department & Location	Tel.
	D. Taylor	Mech. Eng. Workshop	6200
Subject	Preliminary Report, Accident, 12 May		

While turning a brass component on Tuesday, last week, Kenneth Oliver, machinist, received an injury to his eye. He was taken to the Eye Hospital where I understand he was operated on. I believe the accident was due to carelessness.

Language study *Making safety rules*

What are the differences in meaning, if any, between these statements?

1 Wear protective clothing.
2 Always wear protective clothing.
3 Protective clothing must be worn.

We can make safety rules in these ways:

1 Using an imperative.

> **Wear** *protective clothing.*

> **Do not wear** *loose-fitting clothing.*

2 *Always/never* are used to emphasize that the rule holds in all cases.

> **Always** *wear protective clothing.*

> **Never** *wear loose-fitting clothing.*

3 We can use a modal verb for emphasis.

> *Protective clothing* **must** *be worn.*

> *Protective clothing* **should** *be worn.*

Task 6

Study this list of unsafe environmental conditions (hazards). Write safety rules to limit these hazards using the methods given above. For example:

> inadequate lighting

> *Lighting must be adequate.* or
> *Lighting should be adequate.*

1 uneven floors
2 unguarded machinery
3 untidy workbenches
4 untidy workplaces
5 badly maintained machinery
6 carelessly stored dangerous materials
7 inadequate ventilation
8 damaged tools and equipment
9 machinery in poor condition
10 equipment used improperly
11 equipment operated by untrained personnel
12 apprentices working without supervision

Writing *Ways of linking ideas, 2*

In Unit 4 we learnt that to make our writing effective, we have to make sure our readers can follow our ideas. We learnt how to mark reasons, results, and contrasts in our writing.

What are the links between these ideas? What words can we use to mark the links?

1 The accident happened.
2 The operator's carelessness.
3 The supervisor was not present.

Sentence 2 is a *reason* for sentence 1. Sentence 3 is an *additional* reason. We can mark the links between them like this:

> The accident happened **because of** the operator's carelessness. **In addition/moreover**, the supervisor was not present.

We use *because of* to introduce a reason which is a noun or noun phrase. We use *in addition* and *moreover* to introduce an additional reason.

What are the links between these ideas? What words can we use to mark the links?

4   Suitable protection should be worn.
5   Safety helmets should be used where there is a danger of falling objects.

Sentence 5 is an example to illustrate sentence 4. We can mark this in this way:

> Suitable protection should be worn. **For example/For instance**, safety helmets should be used where there is a danger of falling objects.

Task 7

Show the links between these sets of ideas using appropriate linking words from this unit and from Unit 4.

1   Many accidents happen.
    Workers' carelessness.
2   Education can reduce accidents.
    It is important that all workers receive training in basic safety.
3   Eye injuries can be serious.
    Goggles must be worn for grinding and cutting.
4   Safety gloves provide protection for the hands.
    They prevent burns.
    They reduce the danger of cuts.
5   Safety shoes protect the feet against falling objects.
    They prevent the feet getting caught in machinery.
6   Respirators should be worn in dusty conditions.
    Dust can damage the lungs.
7   Safety gear exists for every danger.
    Each year people are injured.
    They refuse or forget to wear the right gear.

10 Young engineer

Tuning-in

Task 1

Lucy Porter is a recent winner of the *Young Engineer for Britain* award. Study this diagram of her invention. Discuss these questions in your group:

1 What is it?
2 Who is it for?
3 How does it work?

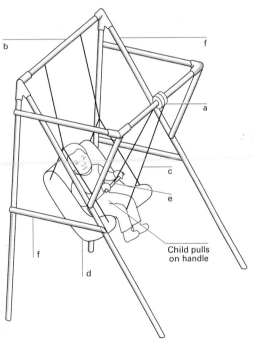

Child pulls
on handle

Listening

Task 2   ⌨   Now listen to Lucy talking about her invention and career plans. As you listen, check your answers to Task 1.

Task 3   ⌨   Now listen again. Here are some of the things Lucy talks about. Put them in the correct sequence. The first one has been done for you.

a	Her career plans.	_____
b	What happens next with her invention.	_____
c	How it works.	_____
d	Why she is planning to study engineering.	_____
e	Changes in the design.	_____
f	What her invention is called.	*1*
g	What materials she used.	_____
h	Who it is intended for.	_____
i	How she made the prototype.	_____
j	How she got the idea.	_____
k	Her views on engineering as a career for women.	_____

Task 4   Now make notes on what Lucy says about the above topics.

Task 5   Label the diagram in Task 1 with these terms:

1 rope
2 handle
3 pulley
4 A-frames
5 cross-piece
6 seat

Task 6   Put these steps in the creation and development of the swing in the correct sequence. The first and last have been done for you.

a	problem identified	*1*
b	prototype built in wood	_____
c	metal version built	_____
d	design modified	_____
e	patent applied for	_____
f	models built to test design	_____
g	prototype modified	_____
h	prototype tested	_____
i	design drawn	_____
j	manufacturer licensed to produce	*10*

Task 7   ⌨   Now listen again and answer these more detailed questions.

1 How did the invention get its name?
2 What did she use to test designs which seemed viable?
3 Why did she make the first swing from wood?
4 What are the advantages of a metal frame?

Writing *Describing and explaining*

You are going to write a brief description and explanation of Lucy's invention. It will consist of two paragraphs.

Paragraph 1
Use the labelled diagram in Task 1 and the information from the tape to write a brief description of Lucy's invention. Your description should answer these questions:

1 What is it called?
2 What is it for?
3 What does it consist of?
4 How are the parts connected?
5 What is it made of?

Use the language of description studied in Unit 6.

Paragraph 2
The following steps explain how the swing works. Put them in the correct sequence. Then use *so* and *when* to link them into a paragraph.

The rope pulls the seat forwards.
Repetition of these actions causes a swinging motion.
The child pulls down on the handle.
The seat swings back under the weight of the child.
The child releases the handle.

Speaking practice

Work in pairs, **A** and **B**.

Student A: Play the part of the interviewer. Base your questions on the topics in Task 3, and any other questions you may wish to add. For example:

a Her career plans. → *What are your career plans?*

Student B: Play the part of the swing inventor.

Conduct the interview.

11 Washing machine

Tuning-in

Task 1

Many items found in the home contain control systems. The washing machine is one of the most complex. List some of the factors the control system of a washing machine must handle. This diagram may help you.

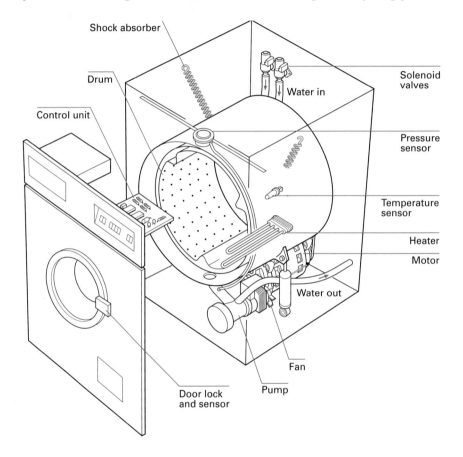

Fig.1 Cross- section through a washing machine

Reading *Reading diagrams*

In engineering, diagrams carry a great deal of information. They can also help you to understand the accompanying text. For this reason, it is helpful to try to understand any diagram before reading the text.

Task 2

Study the diagram again. Try to explain the function of each of these items.

1 Pump
2 Motor

3 Shock absorber
4 Solenoid valves
5 Heater
6 Pressure sensor
7 Door lock and sensor
8 Temperature sensor
9 Fan

Task 3

Read this text to check your answers to Task 1.

Control systems in the home

Most devices in the home have some sort of control. For example, you can control the volume of a TV by using a remote control. The building blocks of a control system are:

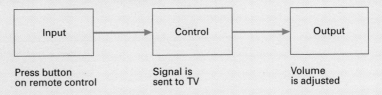

The input can be any movement or any change in the environment.
5 For example, a drop in temperature may cause a heating system to come on.

The control may change the size of the output (for example, adjusting the sound of a TV). Often this involves changing one kind of input into a different kind of output. For example, opening a
10 window may set off a burglar alarm.

Outputs can be of many kinds. An alarm system may ring a bell, flash lights, and send a telephone message to the police.

Most control systems are closed loops. That means they incorporate a way of checking that the output is correct. In other
15 words, they have feedback. The thermostat in a central heating system (Fig. 2) provides constant feedback to the control unit.

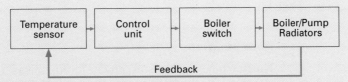

Fig. 2

The control system of a modern washing machine has to take into account several different factors. These are door position, water level, water temperature, wash and spin times, and drum speeds.
20 Most of them are decided when you select which washing program to use.

Fig. 3 shows a block diagram of a washing machine control system. You can see that this is quite a complex closed loop system using feedback to keep a check on water level, water temperature, and
25 drum speeds.

►

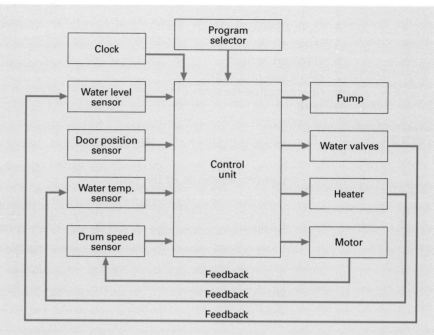

Fig. 3

The control unit is the heart of the system. It receives and sends out signals which control all the activities of the machine. It is also capable of diagnosing faults which may occur, stopping the program, and informing the service engineer what is wrong. It is a
30 small, dedicated computer which, like other computers, uses the language of logic.

Source: P. Fowler and M. Horsley, 'Control systems in the home', *CDT: Technology*

Task 4

Read the following text to find the answers to these questions:

1 What device is used to lock the door?
2 What provides feedback to the control unit about the door position?

Text 1

Door position

The machine will not start any program unless the door is fully closed and locked. When the door is closed, it completes an electrical circuit which heats up a heat-sensitive pellet. This expands as it gets hot, pushing a mechanical lock into place and
5 closing a switch. The switch signals the control unit that the door is closed and locked. Only when it has received this signal will the control unit start the wash program.

Now work in pairs, **A** and **B**.

Student A: Read Texts 2 and 3.
Student B: Read Texts 4 and 5.

Complete your section of the table opposite. Then exchange information with your partner to complete the whole table.

	Control factor	Operating device	Feedback by
1	Door position	heat-sensitive pellet	switch
2	Water level		
3	Water temperature		
4	Wash and spin times		—
5	Drum speeds		

Text 2

Water level

When a wash program first starts it has to open the valves which allow the water in. There are usually two of these valves, one for hot water and one for cold. Each must be controlled separately depending on the water temperature needed for that program. The
5 valves are solenoid operated, i.e. they are opened and closed electrically.

The rising water level is checked by the water level sensor. This is a pressure sensor. The pressure of the air in the plastic tube rises as it is compressed by the rising water. The pressure sensor keeps the
10 control unit informed as to the pressure reached and the control unit uses the information to decide when to close the water inlet valves.

Text 3

Water temperature

The temperature sensor, a type of thermometer which fits inside the washer drum, measures the water temperature and signals it to the control unit. The control unit compares it with the temperature needed for the program being used. If the water temperature is too
5 low, the control unit will switch on the heater. The temperature sensor continues to check the temperature and keep the control unit informed. Once the correct temperature is reached, the control unit switches off the heater and moves on to the next stage of the program.

Text 4

Clock

The control unit includes a memory which tells it how long each stage of a program should last. The times may be different for each program. The electronic clock built into the control unit keeps the memory of the control unit informed so that each stage of each
5 program is timed correctly.

Text 5

> **Drum speed**
>
> During the washing and spinning cycles of the program, the drum has to spin at various speeds. Most machines use three different speeds: 53 rpm for washing; 83 rpm for distributing the load before spinning; 100 rpm for spinning.
>
> 5   The control unit signals the motor to produce these speeds. The motor starts up slowly, then gradually increases speed. The speed sensor, a tachogenerator, keeps the control unit informed as to the speed that has been reached. The control unit uses the information to control the power to the motor and so controls the speed of the
> 10   drum at all times.

Language study   *If/Unless* sentences

Task 5

Fill in the blanks in this table using the information in Fig. 3 and the texts in Task 4.

Sensor	Condition	Control unit action
Water	level low	open inlet valves
	level high enough	_____
Water temperature	_____	switch on heater
	high enough	_____
Drum speed	_____	_____
	_____	decrease motor speed

The conditions which the sensors report determine the action of the control unit. We can link each condition and action like this:

> **If** *the water level is low, the inlet valves are opened.*

Task 6

Write similar sentences for the other five conditions given.

Now study this example:

Sensor	Condition	Control unit action
Door	Door open	Machine cannot start
	Door closed	Machine can start

We can link these conditions and actions as follows:

1   **If** *the door is open, the machine cannot start.*

2   **If** *the door is closed, the machine can start.*

3   **Unless** *the door is closed, the machine cannot start.*

We use *unless* when an action cannot or will not happen if a prior condition is not true. In example 3, *Unless* means *If ... not*. We can rewrite 3 as:

> **If** *the door is **not** closed, the machine cannot start.*

Complete these sentences using *Unless* and your knowledge of engineering.

1 Unless the ignition is switched on, a car cannot_____.

2 Unless the pilot light is on, gas central heating will not_____.

3 Unless the diverter valve is switched to central heating, the radiators will not

_____.

4 Unless there is current flowing in the primary coil of a transformer, there will

be no current in the_____ coil.

5 Unless there is_____ in the cylinders, a petrol engine will not start.

6 Unless the doors are_____, a lift will not operate.

7 Unless mild steel is painted, it will_____.

8 Unless electrical equipment is earthed, it may be_____.

Writing *Explaining a diagram*

Task 8

Study this diagram of a pressure sensor. Explain how it works by linking each
pair of actions with appropriate time words.

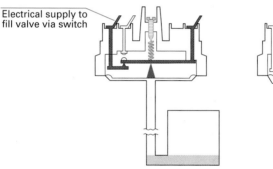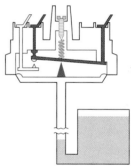

Electrical supply to
fill valve via switch

1 A wash programme first starts.
  It opens the valves to allow the water in.
2 The water level in the drum rises.
  The air in the plastic tube is compressed.
3 The pressure rises.
  The diaphragm moves upwards.
4 This continues.
  The switch contacts are separated.
5 This happens.
  The fill valves are closed.

Task 9

Join the following groups of statements to make longer sentences. Use the words printed in *italics* above each group. You may omit words and make whatever changes you think are necessary in the word order and punctuation of the sentences. Join the sentences to make a paragraph.

1 *which*
The temperature sensor measures the water temperature.
The temperature sensor is a type of thermometer.

2 *and*
The temperature sensor fits inside the washer drum.
The temperature sensor signals the water temperature to the control unit.

3 *which*
The control unit compares the water temperature with the temperature.
The temperature is needed for the programme being used.

4 *If*
The water temperature is too low.
The control unit will switch on the heater.

5 *and*
The temperature sensor continues to check the temperature.
The temperature sensor keeps the control unit informed.

6 *When ... and*
The correct temperature is reached.
The control unit switches off the heater.
The control unit moves on to the next stage of the programme.

12 Racing bicycle

Chris Boardman in the 1992 Olympics.

Tuning-in

Task 1

Label this diagram of a bicycle with these terms.

pedals	chain	chain-wheel
seat	gears	brakes
handlebars	frame	toe-clips

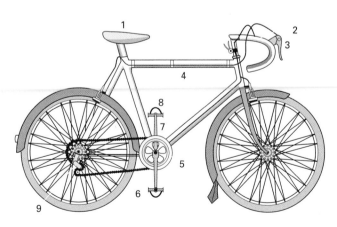

Fig. 1

Task 2 ⌨ Check your answers by listening to this description.

Compare Fig. 2 (below) with the bicycle shown in Fig. 1 and Task 2. What differences can you note? Write your answers in this table.

Conventional (Fig. 1)	**Improvement** (Fig. 2)
Spoked wheels	
Gear lever on the frame	
Tubular aluminium-alloy frame	
Pedals with toe-clips	
Steel gears	
Ordinary handlebars	

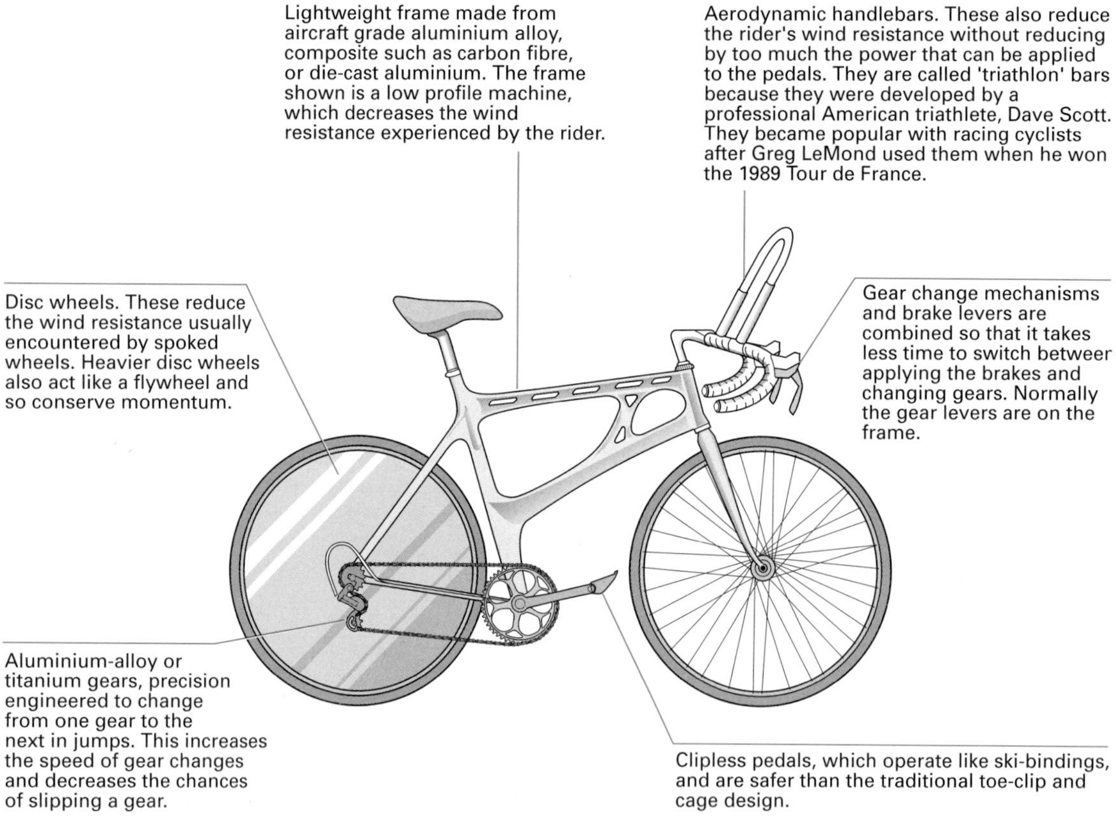

Lightweight frame made from aircraft grade aluminium alloy, composite such as carbon fibre, or die-cast aluminium. The frame shown is a low profile machine, which decreases the wind resistance experienced by the rider.

Aerodynamic handlebars. These also reduce the rider's wind resistance without reducing by too much the power that can be applied to the pedals. They are called 'triathlon' bars because they were developed by a professional American triathlete, Dave Scott. They became popular with racing cyclists after Greg LeMond used them when he won the 1989 Tour de France.

Disc wheels. These reduce the wind resistance usually encountered by spoked wheels. Heavier disc wheels also act like a flywheel and so conserve momentum.

Gear change mechanisms and brake levers are combined so that it takes less time to switch betweer applying the brakes and changing gears. Normally the gear levers are on the frame.

Aluminium-alloy or titanium gears, precision engineered to change from one gear to the next in jumps. This increases the speed of gear changes and decreases the chances of slipping a gear.

Clipless pedals, which operate like ski-bindings, and are safer than the traditional toe-clip and cage design.

Fig. 2

Check your answers to Task 3 in column 1 opposite. Then study Fig. 2 again to find reasons for each improvement.

Improvement	Reason
Disc wheels	
Combined gear change and brake levers	
Carbon fibre frame	
Clipless pedals	
Precision-engineered aluminium-alloy or titanium gears	
Aerodynamic handlebars	

Reading *Prediction*

Task 5

Study this extract from the text you are going to read.

> Bicycles, and especially racing bicycles, have much in common with aircraft:

What similarities between racing bicycles and aircraft do you think the text will cover? Note your predictions.

Task 6

Read this text to check your answers to Task 5.

Racing bicycle

The standard design of the bicycle has been in existence for about 100 years. But in the past 10 years there have been more changes than during any other decade.

Bicycles, and especially racing bicycles, have much in common
5 with aircraft: both are designed to minimize wind resistance, maximize energy efficiency, respond instantly to the demands placed on them, yet weigh very little without losing strength. So, much of the technology used in aerospace has found its way into racing bicycles.

10 The heart of the bicycle is its frame. It must be strong, light, flexible enough to absorb bumps, but not so much that it wastes the energy the rider transmits by pedalling.

Bicycle frame designers share many aims with aircraft engineers, who must design wings which are strong, light, aerodynamic, and
15 efficient at converting engine power into lift. Yet the wings must be flexible enough to absorb turbulence without wasting the engine's thrust. Therefore, the modern bicycle frame and aircraft wing share both materials and design features. Many racing bicycle frames which consist of tubes joined together are made from aluminium
20 alloys similar to those used in aviation. The French company, Vitus, ▶

glues the tubes together using the same techniques as those used for connecting aircraft components.

In recent years, aircraft manufacturers such as Boeing have been experimenting with composite materials like Cheval and carbon
25 fibres. It is no surprise that some racing bicycle frames are now manufactured from the same materials.

Perhaps the most innovative frame to date is constructed from die-cast magnesium alloy. Its designer, Frank Kirk, formerly worked in aerospace.

30 Components which fit on bicycle frames have also benefited from aerospace engineering. Many components, such as gears, brakes, handlebars, and wheels, are both aerodynamic and often made from aluminium alloys or titanium – another light, strong metal used in aircraft.

Language study *Describing reasons*

We can describe the reasons for an improvement or design change in a number of ways. Study this example:

Improvement/Design change	Reason
Disc wheels	Reduce wind resistance.

How many ways do you know to link an improvement and the reason for it? Try to complete this sentence by adding the reason given.

New racing bicycles have disc wheels _____.

Using *to* + verb is the easiest way to link improvement and reason. For example:

*New racing bicycles have disc wheels **to** reduce wind resistance.*

Another simple way is to use a linking word. You studied this in Unit 5. For example:

*New racing bicycles have disc wheels **because**/**since**/**as** this reduces wind resistance.*

A more difficult way is to use *so that* which must be followed by a clause. For example:

*New racing bicycles have disc wheels **so that** wind resistance is reduced.*

Task 7

Link each improvement and reason in Task 4 using the methods given above.

Writing *Describing contrast*

In engineering, it is often necessary to compare and contrast different proposals, solutions to problems, and developments. In this unit we will focus on contrast – describing differences.

We can show differences in a table like this:

Conventional	Improved bicycle
Spoked wheels	Disc wheels
Gear lever on the frame	Combined gear change and brake levers
Tubular aluminium-alloy frame	Carbon fibre frame
Pedals with toe-clips	Clipless pedals
Steel gears	Precision-engineered titanium gears
Ordinary handlebars	Aerodynamic handlebars

We can describe differences using:

1   the comparative form of the adjective or adverb. For example:

*The new bicycle **is lighter than** the old.*
*The new bicycle **is more aerodynamic than** the old.*
*Titanium gears can be changed **more easily**.*

2   the connecting words *but/whereas, in contrast*. For example:

*On new bicycles the gear and brake lever are combined, **whereas** on old ones, the gear lever is on the frame.*
*Old bicycles have spoked wheels. **In contrast**, the new bicycle has disc wheels.*

3   using expressions such as *unlike/different from*. For example:

***Unlike** the conventional bicycle, the new bicycle has a carbon fibre frame.*
*The new bicycle is **different from** the conventional one in that the gears are made of titanium.*

Note that these expressions assume that the reader is familiar with the materials used in the conventional bicycle, which are not mentioned.

Task 8   Describe the differences between a conventional and an improved bicycle using the information in the table above and appropriate expressions from the list provided.

Word study *Properties of materials*

Study these examples of adjective and noun pairs for describing the properties of materials.

Adjective	Noun
flexible	flexibility
light	lightness
strong	strength

Task 9　　Now fill in the gaps in this table with the missing adjectives and nouns.

Adjective	Noun
_____	wind resistance
elastic	_____
_____	plasticity
tough	_____
soft	_____
rigid	_____
wear-resistant	_____
_____	brittleness
hard	_____

Speaking practice

Task 10　　Work in pairs, **A** and **B**.

Student A: Your task is to explain to your partner how to adjust the distance between the saddle and the handlebars of a racing bicycle. Use the text and diagrams on pages 177/8 to help you.

Student B: Your task is to explain to your partner how to adjust the height and tilt of the handlebars of a racing bicycle. Use the text and diagrams on pages 181/2 to help you.

Technical reading　*Gear systems*

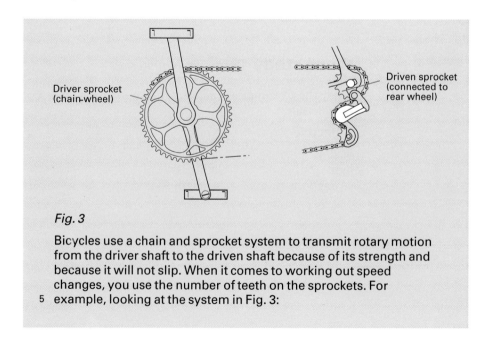

Driver sprocket (chain-wheel)

Driven sprocket (connected to rear wheel)

Fig. 3

Bicycles use a chain and sprocket system to transmit rotary motion from the driver shaft to the driven shaft because of its strength and because it will not slip. When it comes to working out speed changes, you use the number of teeth on the sprockets. For
5　example, looking at the system in Fig. 3:

Driver sprocket has 60 teeth.

Driven sprocket has 15 teeth.

Number of teeth on driven sprocket

Gear speed ratio =   ÷

Number of teeth on driver sprocket

= $\frac{15}{60}$ or 1:4

Task 11

Calculate the gear ratios of a bicycle with the system shown in Fig. 4 below. It has a double chain-wheel and five driven sprockets on the rear wheel but only the combinations shown below are recommended. You may need a calculator.

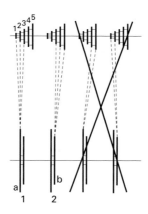

Fig. 4

Chain-wheel	teeth	Sprocket	teeth	Ratio
a	51	1	15	1:3.4
		2	17	_____
		3	21	_____
b	42	3	21	_____
		4	24	_____
		5	28	_____

13 Lasers

Tuning-in

Task 1

What are lasers? List any applications you know for lasers.

Reading

Task 2

Read this text to check your answers to Task 1.

Lasers (Light Amplification by Stimulated Emission of Radiation) are devices which amplify light and produce beams of light which are very intense, directional, and pure in colour. They can be solid state, gas, semiconductor, or liquid.

5 When lasers were invented in 1960, some people thought they could be used as 'death rays'. In the 1980s, the United States experimented with lasers as a defence against nuclear missiles. Nowadays, they are used to identify targets. But apart from military uses, they have many applications in engineering,
10 communications, medicine, and the arts.

In engineering, powerful laser beams can be focused on a small area. These beams can heat, melt, or vaporize material in a very precise way. They can be used for drilling diamonds, cutting complex shapes in materials from plastics to steel, for spot welding
15 and for surfacing techniques, such as hardening aircraft engine turbine blades. Laser beams can also be used to measure and align structures.

Lasers are ideal for communications in space. Laser light can carry many more information channels than microwaves because of its
20 high frequency. In addition, it can travel long distances without

losing signal strength. Lasers can also be used for information recording and reading. Compact discs are read by lasers.

25 In medicine, laser beams can treat damaged tissue in a fraction of a second without harming healthy tissue. They can be used in very precise eye operations.

In the arts, lasers can provide fantastic displays of light. Pop concerts are often accompanied by laser displays.

Task 3

Complete this table of laser applications using information from the text opposite. You may also add any applications you know of which are not included in the text.

Military	Engineering	Communications	Medicine	Arts
_____	drilling diamonds	_____	treating damaged tissue	_____
	cutting complex shapes	information recording and reading		
	_____		_____	
	_____			
	_____			
	_____			

Language study *used to/for*

Study these examples of laser applications:

1   Laser beams can be *used to measure* and align structures.

2   They can be *used for drilling* diamonds.

3   They can be *used for* light displays.

We can describe applications with *used to* + infinitive or *used for* + *-ing* or noun.

Task 4

Describe the applications of lasers using the information in your table in Task 3 and the structures given above.

Word study *Noun + noun compounds*

We can use adjectives to describe an object in greater detail. For example:

light	*electric light*
a motor	*an electric motor*
steel	*stainless steel*
gears	*helical gears*

We can also use nouns. For example:

light	*laser light*
a motor	*an air motor*
steel	*carbon steel*
gears	*titanium gears*

Many relationships are possible in noun compounds. For example:

an air motor	a motor which uses air
carbon steel	steel which contains carbon
titanium gears	gears made of titanium

Task 5

Put each of these examples in the correct column.

carbon blocks	a power tool
aluminium alloy	a ball bearing
carbon fibre	a concrete beam
a gas burner	a diesel boat
roller bearings	a spring balance
a circuit board	a plastic tube
a plastic pipe	steel sheets
magnesium alloy	

uses	is made of	contains

Task 6

What new relationships can you find in the examples below? Rewrite each compound to show the relationship. For example:

a foot pump	*a pump which is operated by foot*
a ribbon cable	*a cable which is like a ribbon*
a gear lever	*a lever for operating gears*

1	chain wheel		**6**	college lecturer
2	disc wheel		**7**	toe-clip
3	foot brake		**8**	boiler thermostat
4	a hand throttle		**9**	safety helmet
5	strain gauge		**10**	aircraft engineer

Writing *Describing a process, 1: sequence*

When we write about a process, we have to:

1   Sequence the stages

2   Locate the stages

3   Describe what happens at each stage

4   Explain what happens at each stage

In this unit, we will study how to sequence the stages.

Consider these stages in the operation of a washing machine.

1 The drum is filled with water.
2 The water is heated to the right temperature.
3 Soap is added.
4 The drum is rotated slowly.
5 The dirty water is pumped out.
6 Clean water is added.
7 The drum is rotated much faster and the water pumped out.
8 The clean clothes are removed.

Instead of numbers, we can show the correct order using sequence words.

First the drum is filled with water.
Then the water is heated to the right temperature.
Next soap is added.
After that, the drum is rotated slowly.
Next the dirty water is pumped out.
Then clean water is added.
After that, the drum is rotated much faster and the water pumped out.
Finally, the clean clothes are removed.

Task 7

Study this diagram. It shows an extruder for forming plastic pipes. Describe the extruder.

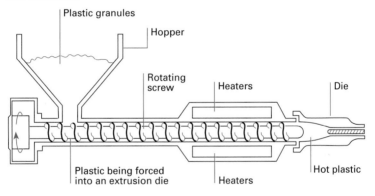

Task 8

Now put these stages in the process in the correct sequence.

a The hot plastic is forced through the die to form a continuous length of pipe.
b The rotating screw forces the plastic past heaters.
c The plastic granules are mixed and placed in the hopper.
d The pipe is cooled and cut to suitable lengths.
e The plastic melts.

Task 9

Describe the correct order using sequence words. Add to your description of the process your description of the extruder from Task 7. Form your text into a paragraph.

Technical reading *Laser cutting*

Engineers have to read sales literature describing the products and services of companies. Read the following sales literature to answer these questions:

1 Who is this text for?
2 What service does the company provide?
3 What are the design benefits of laser cutting?
4 Can lasers cut non-metals?
5 What limitations are there on the service they provide?
6 How does the service cut lead time?

DESIGN ENGINEERS – DEVELOPMENT ENGINEERS – BUYERS – STOCK CONTROLLERS

Frustrated?

By having to restrict designs to suit manufacturing processes?
By the difficulty and high cost of producing accurate prototypes?
By the high cost and lengthy lead times associated with press tools?
By the high stock levels necessitated by minimum batch sizes?

If your answer to any of the above is yes ...

WE HAVE THE SOLUTION!
OUR NEW 1500 WATT CNC-CONTROLLED LASER CUTTER IS AT YOUR DISPOSAL.

■ The Process

Laser technology is not new, but it is only recently that the full benefits have become available to manufacturers.

Taking light and passing it through a series of lenses makes the light source so great that its power density is several million times that of the sun – this laser energy is then used to cut almost any material.

The light is directed down towards a CNC-controlled table making it very easy to produce accurate complicated shapes without distortion, giving burr-free, smooth, and perfectly square edges.

■ The Materials
The laser is suitable for cutting:

– All types of steel including stainless and spring steel.

– Most non-ferrous metals.

– Plastics, wood, fibreglass, and almost any other material you care to mention!

■ The Capacity
Carbon Steel – up to 13 mm
Stainless Steel – up to 10 mm
Plastics – up to 40 mm
Wood – up to 40 mm
Rubber – up to 40 mm
Table movement 1650 mm x 1250 mm

■ The Advantages
Short lead time
No tooling costs
Low set-up costs
Extremely accurate
Highest quality
Minimal heat affected zones
Design flexibility

Source: Eraba Limited

14 Automation technician

Tuning-in

Task 1

You are going to hear an interview with Alistair, a technician with an American company based in the United Kingdom. His company produces cellular communication equipment. Try to list some of the products his company might make.

Listening

Task 2

Listen to Part 1 of the interview. Check your answers to Task 1 and answer these questions.

1 What is his job title?
2 What does his section build?
3 What type of machines are they?
4 What does a Fuji robot do?
5 What do his machines do?
6 What three types of sensors does a robot have?

Task 3 ⊡ Listen to Part 2 of the interview and answer these questions.

1 How long has he been with the company?
2 How many technicians are in his section?
3 When does he start work?
4 What does he do first when he gets to work?
5 Name one thing he might do after that.
6 Why does he visit plants in Europe?
7 Where has he been?
8 What does he dislike about travelling?

Task 4 ⊡ Listen to Part 3 of the interview and answer these questions.

1 What did the company he previously worked for make?
2 Name one thing he feels was good about working for his old company.
3 What qualification does he have?
4 How long did it take to get this qualification?
5 During his work placement, what did he do a lot of?
6 What kind of companies did he do installations in?
7 What was one of the perks of the job?

Task 5 ⊡ Listen to the interview again and complete the gaps in this record of Alistair's work experience.

Period	Type of company	Product	Job title
2 years	_____	_____	Automation technician
_____ years	_____	Telephone exchange	_____
_____ months	Instrument makers	_____	Student placement

Speaking practice *Talking about specifications*

Task 6 Work in pairs, **A** and **B**. Some of the design specifications for your drawing are missing. Complete them with help from your partner.

Before you start, make sure you know how to say these abbreviations and expressions in full:

1 max. maximum
2 min. minimum
3 dia. diameter
4 cm centimetre
5 kg kilogram
6 1.42 one point four two
7 0.55 zero point five five
8 ± plus or minus

You may look at each other's drawings after you have exchanged information.

Student A: Your specifications are on page 178.
Student B: Your specifications are on page 182.

15 Refrigerator

Tuning-in

Task 1

Study this diagram. It explains how a refrigerator works. In your group try to work out the function of each of the numbered components using the information in the diagram.

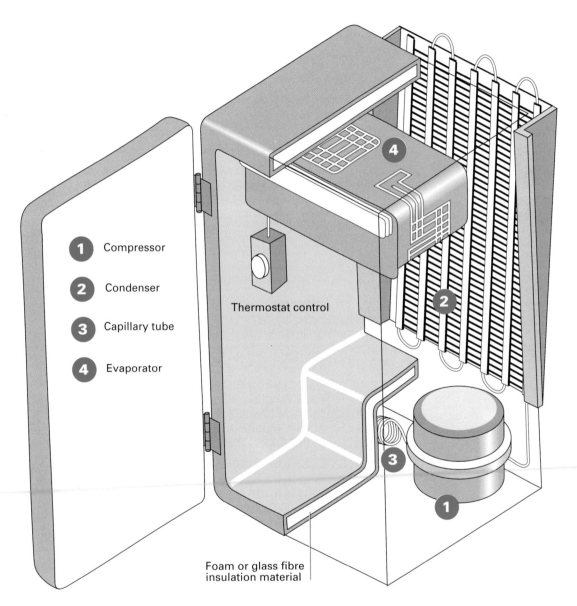

1 Compressor

2 Condenser

3 Capillary tube

4 Evaporator

Thermostat control

Foam or glass fibre insulation material

Reading *Dealing with unfamiliar words, 1*

You are going to read a text about refrigerators. Your purpose is to find out how they operate. Read the first paragraph of the text below. Underline any words which are unfamiliar to you.

> Refrigeration preserves food by lowering its temperature. It slows down the growth and reproduction of micro-organisms such as bacteria and the action of enzymes which cause food to rot.

You may have underlined words like *micro-organisms*, *bacteria*, or *enzymes*. These are words which are uncommon in engineering. Before you look them up in a dictionary or try to find translations in your own language, think! Do you need to know the meaning of these words to understand how refrigerators operate?

You can ignore unfamiliar words which do not help you to achieve your reading purpose.

Task 2

Now read the text to check your explanation of how a refrigerator works. Ignore any unfamiliar words which will not help you to achieve this purpose.

Fridge

para

Refrigeration preserves food by lowering its temperature. It slows *1*
down the growth and reproduction of micro-organisms such as
bacteria and the action of enzymes which cause food to rot.

Refrigeration is based on three principles. Firstly, if a liquid is *2*
5 heated, it changes to a gas or vapour. When this gas is cooled, it
changes back into a liquid. Secondly, if a gas is allowed to expand,
it cools down. If a gas is compressed, it heats up. Thirdly, lowering
the pressure around a liquid helps it to boil.

To keep the refrigerator at a constant low temperature, heat must *3*
10 be transferred from the inside of the cabinet to the outside. A
refrigerant is used to do this. It is circulated around the fridge,
where it undergoes changes in pressure and temperature and
changes from a liquid to a gas and back again.

One common refrigerant is a compound of carbon, chlorine, and *4*
15 fluorine known as R12. This has a very low boiling point: −29°C. At
normal room temperature (about 20°C) the liquid quickly turns into
gas. However, newer refrigerants which are less harmful to the
environment, such as KLEA 134a, are gradually replacing R12.

The refrigeration process begins in the compressor. This *5*
20 compresses the gas so that it heats up. It then pumps the gas into a
condenser, a long tube in the shape of a zigzag. As the warm gas
passes through the condenser, it heats the surroundings and cools
down. By the time it leaves the condenser, it has condensed back
into a liquid.

25 Liquid leaving the condenser has to flow down a very narrow tube *6*
(a capillary tube). This prevents liquid from leaving the condenser
too quickly, and keeps it at a high pressure.

▶

As the liquid passes from the narrow capillary tube to the larger   7
tubes of the evaporator, the pressure quickly drops. The liquid
30 turns to vapour, which expands and cools. The cold vapour
absorbs heat from the fridge. It is then sucked back into the
compressor and the process begins again.

The compressor is switched on and off by a thermostat, a device   8
that regulates temperature, so that the food is not over-frozen.

Source: 'Inside out: Fridge', *Education Guardian*

Language study *Principles and laws*

Study these extracts from the text above. What kind of statements are they?

1   If a liquid is heated, it changes to a gas or vapour.

2   If a gas is allowed to expand, it cools down.

3   If a gas is compressed, it heats up.

Each consists of an action followed by a result. For example:

Action	*Result*
a liquid is heated	it changes to a gas or vapour

These statements are principles. They describe things in science and engineering which are always true. The action is always followed by the same result.

Principles have this form:

If/When (action – present tense), (result – present tense).

Task 3

Link each action in column **A** with a result from column **B** to describe an important engineering principle.

A Action	B Result
1 a liquid is heated	**a** it heats up
2 a gas is cooled	**b** there is an equal and opposite
3 a gas expands	reaction
4 a gas is compressed	**c** it changes to a gas
5 a force is applied to a body	**d** it extends in proportion to the force
6 a current passes through a wire	**e** it is transmitted equally throughout
7 a wire cuts a magnetic field	the fluid
8 pressure is applied to the surface	**f** a current is induced in the wire
of an enclosed fluid	**g** it cools down
9 a force is applied to a spring fixed	**h** it sets up a magnetic field around the
at one end	wire
	i it changes to a liquid

Word study *Verbs and related nouns*

Task 4

Each of the verbs in column **A** has a related noun ending in *-er* or *-or* in column **B**. Complete the blanks. You have studied these words in this and earlier units. Use a dictionary to check any spellings which you are not certain about.

A Verbs	**B Nouns**
For example:	
refrigerate	refrigerator
1 condense	_____
2 _____	evaporator
3 compress	_____
4 resist	_____
5 _____	charger
6 generate	_____
7 conduct	_____
8 _____	exchanger
9 radiate	_____
10 control	_____

Writing *Describing a process, 2: location*

Study this diagram. It describes the refrigeration process.

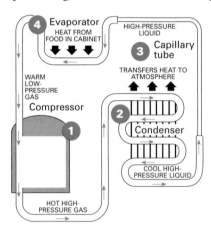

In Unit 13 we learnt that when we write about a process, we have to:

1   Sequence the stages

2   Locate the stages

3   Describe what happens at each stage

4   Explain what happens at each stage

For example:

sequence location   description

The refrigeration process begins in the compressor. This compresses the gas

explanation
so that it heats up.

In this unit we will study ways to locate the stages.

Task 5

Put these stages in the refrigeration process in the correct sequence with the help of the diagram above. The first one has been done for you.

a   The liquid enters the evaporator.   _____

b   The gas condenses back into a liquid.   _____

c   The vapour is sucked back into the compressor. _____

d   The gas is compressed.   *1*

e   The liquid turns into a vapour.   _____

f   The gas passes through the condenser.   _____

g   The liquid passes through a capillary tube.   _____

h   The high pressure is maintained.   _____

There are two ways to locate a stage in a process.

1   Using a preposition + noun phrase. For example:

*The liquid turns to vapour **in the evaporator**.*
*The gas cools down **in the condenser**.*

2   Using a *where*-clause, a relative clause with *where* rather than *which* or *who*, to link a stage, its location, and what happens there. For example:

*The warm gas passes through the condenser, **where it heats the surroundings and cools down**.*
*The refrigerant circulates around the fridge, **where it undergoes changes in pressure and temperature**.*

Task 6

Complete each of these statements.

1   The gas passes through the compressor, where _____.

2   It passes through the condenser, where _____.

3   The liquid passes through a capillary tube, where _____.

4   The liquid enters the evaporator, where _____.

5   The cold vapour is sucked back into the compressor, where _____.

Task 7

Add sequence expressions to your statements to show the correct order of events. For example:

First the gas passes through the condenser ...

Make your statements into a paragraph adding extra information from the text in Task 2 if you wish. Then compare your paragraph with paragraphs 6, 7, and 8 from the text.

16 Scales

Tuning-in

Complete this table of common quantities and forces to be measured in engineering, the units in which they are measured, and the instruments you use to measure them.

	Quantity/Force	Unit	Instrument
1	Current	_____	Ammeter
2	_____	Newton	Force gauge
3	Velocity	km/hr	_____
4	_____	°C	Thermometer
5	Thickness	_____	Micrometer
6	_____	Ohm	Ohmmeter
7	Voltage	_____	_____
8	Pressure	_____	Manometer

How can you measure weight accurately? What alternatives are there? If you cannot name the instruments, draw them.

Task 3

What do you think are the advantages of electronic scales over mechanical scales?

Reading 1 *Meaning from context*

Task 4

Read the first two paragraphs of this text and try to fill in the missing words. More than one answer is possible for some of the blanks. Then check your answer to Task 3 using the completed text.

Electronic scales

para

The electronic kitchen scale ¹_____ take a larger load and is   *1*

²_____ accurate than its mechanical counterpart. Whereas a

³_____ scale may have a capacity of about 3kg, broken ⁴_____

25g units, the electronic scale can ⁵_____ a

load of ⁶_____ to 5kg broken into units of 5g or even 2g.

The scale ⁷_____ by converting the load increase on its   *2*

platform ⁸_____ weighing area into a weight reading

⁹_____ the liquid crystal display (LCD). It is controlled ¹⁰_____ a

microprocessor and can therefore ¹¹_____

from ounces to grams at the touch of a button. The compact internal

components also make it small and ¹²_____ to store.

Reading 2 *Comparing sources*

When we read, we may wish to look at more than one source of information on a topic to:

  1   get extra information

  2   find a text we can understand

  3   check points where texts disagree

In the tasks which follow, we will compare information from a diagram and a text.

Task 5   Study this diagram of electronic scales and complete the notes below.

	1 *Load cell*	**2** *Strain gauge*	**3** *Circuit board*
Material	_____	_____	Converter function _____
Position	between the platform and base	_____	Microprocessor function _____
Operation	_____	bends with the load cell, stretching the wires, voltage falls in proportion to load	

The electronic kitchen scale uses microchip technology. It is small, convenient to store, and more accurate than the traditional mechanical scale.

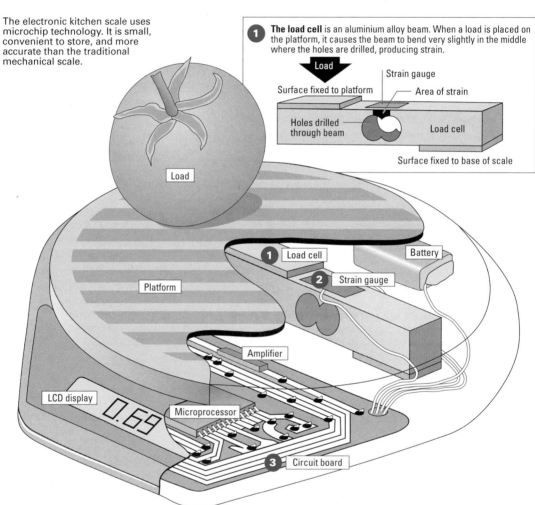

1 **The load cell** is an aluminium alloy beam. When a load is placed on the platform, it causes the beam to bend very slightly in the middle where the holes are drilled, producing strain.

Load

Surface fixed to platform

Strain gauge

Area of strain

Holes drilled through beam

Load cell

Surface fixed to base of scale

Load

Platform

Load cell

Battery

Strain gauge

Amplifier

LCD display   0.69   Microprocessor

Circuit board

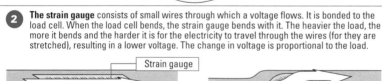

2 **The strain gauge** consists of small wires through which a voltage flows. It is bonded to the load cell. When the load cell bends, the strain gauge bends with it. The heavier the load, the more it bends and the harder it is for the electricity to travel through the wires (for they are stretched), resulting in a lower voltage. The change in voltage is proportional to the load.

Strain gauge

ELECTRICITY

Load cell

ELECTRICITY

Load cell

3 **The circuit board** contains two important components: an analogue to digital converter which amplifies the voltage from the strain gauge and converts it into digital information, and the microprocessor. This changes the digital information into weight which is displayed on the LCD.

Task 6

Scan this text to find information on the load cell, the strain gauge, and the circuit board. Note any information in the text which is new, i.e. additional or different to the information obtained from the diagram.

para

Electronic scales use a weighing device called a load cell underneath the platform. The load cell, an aluminium alloy beam, eliminates the need for springs, cogs, or other moving parts which can wear, break, or cause inaccuracy in mechanical scales.   3

5   A strain gauge is bonded on the load cell. The strain gauge consists of a small piece of metal foil which detects any bending of the beam. A controlled input voltage is supplied to the strain gauge from a battery-powered circuit.   4

When a load is placed on the platform, it causes the load cell to bend very slightly. This, in turn, causes a change in strain, which triggers a change in the electrical resistance of the strain gauge.   5

10

As the resistance changes, so does the output voltage from the strain gauge. In short, the change in voltage across the strain gauge is proportional to the load on the platform.   6

15 The voltage from the gauge is small and has to be amplified and then converted into a digital signal. This signal is fed to a specially programmed microprocessor, which converts it into a weight reading. This is displayed on the LCD. The display will automatically switch off a few minutes after weighing is finished,   7

20 thereby saving battery power.

Source: 'Inside out: Electronic scales', *Education Guardian*

Language study *Cause and effect, 1*

Study these actions. What is the relationship between them?

1   A load is placed on the platform.

2   The load cell bends very slightly.

3   The strain gauge is stretched.

4   The electrical resistance increases.

In each case, the first action is the cause and the second action is the effect. We can link a cause and effect like this:

1+2   *A load is placed on the platform, which **causes** the load cell **to** bend very slightly.*

3+4   *The strain gauge is stretched, which **causes** the electrical resistance **to** increase.*

In these examples, both the cause and the effect are clauses – they contain a subject and a verb. Study this example:

Cause: *The strain gauge is stretched.*
Effect: *An increase in electrical resistance.*

The effect is a noun phrase. We can link cause and effect like this:

*The strain gauge is stretched, which **causes** an increase in electrical resistance.*

In Unit 22 we will study other ways to link a cause and an effect.

The diagram below is a cause and effect chain which explains how a strain gauge works. Each arrow shows a cause and effect link. Match these actions with the correct boxes in the diagram.

a An increase in resistance.
b A load is placed on the scale.
c A drop in voltage across the gauge.
d The load cell bends very slightly.
e They become longer and thinner.
f The strain gauge conductors stretch.
g The strain gauge bends.

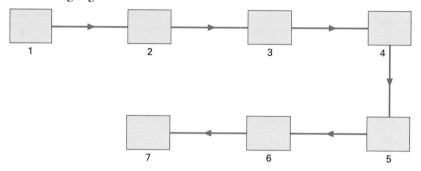

Now practise linking each pair of actions, i.e. 1+2, 2+3, and so on.

Technical reading *Strain gauges*

Read the text below to find the answers to these questions.

1 What principle do strain gauges operate on?
2 Why is it an advantage to have a long length of conductor formed into many rows in a strain gauge?
3 If you want to measure strain in a member, how do you position the strain gauge?
4 Why is an amplifier necessary?
5 Why is a dummy gauge included in the circuit?
6 What is the function of VR2?
7 Why would you adjust the output to exactly zero?
8 In the circuit shown, how is the amplifier output displayed?

> **Strain gauges**
>
> Strain gauges measure the amount of strain in a member. They work on the principle that the electrical resistance of a wire changes as it is stretched, becoming longer and thinner. The more it is stretched, the greater its resistance. Mathematically, this is written
> 5 as:
>
> $$\text{Resistance} \propto \frac{\text{Length}}{\text{Area}} \quad \text{or} \quad R \propto \frac{L}{A}$$
>
> By arranging the wire in tightly packed rows, quite long lengths can be fitted on to a small pad (Fig. 1). Modern strain gauges are made not of wire, but by etching a pattern into metal foil which is stuck to a polyester backing (Fig. 2). ▶

10 In use, a gauge is stuck on to the surface of the member being tested. Its active axis is fixed along the direction in which you want to measure the strain. Movements on the passive axis will have no real effect on it. The gauge must then be connected to an electronic circuit. Fig. 3 shows a block diagram of the complete circuit. The

15 resistance of the gauge is compared with the resistance of fixed value resistors in the circuit. Any differences in resistance are converted into voltage differences. These very small changes in voltage are amplified before being displayed.

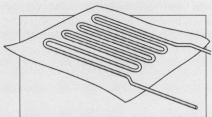

Fig. 1 strain gauge

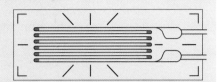

Fig. 2 modern strain gauge

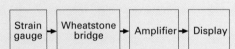

Fig. 3 block diagram of the complete circuit

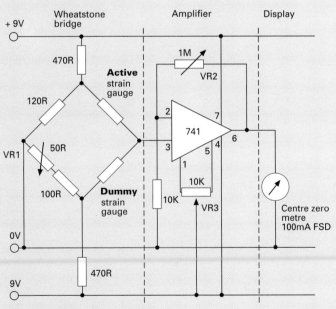

Fig. 4 strain gauge in circuit

The final circuit, shown in Fig. 4, includes a dummy gauge. This

20 compensates for any changes in the resistance of the active gauge caused by temperature changes. The active and dummy gauges form part of the Wheatstone bridge. With no forces applied to the active gauge the output from this part of the circuit should be zero. When forces are applied, the resistance of the active gauge

25 changes so the output voltage to the amplifier changes. The

►

amplifier magnifies that change so that it can be clearly seen on the meter. The three variable resistors in the circuit each allow different adjustments to be made. VR1 allows you to 'balance' the bridge, getting the resistances exactly equal. VR2 allows you to adjust the
30 'gain' of the amplifier, in other words, how much the voltage is amplified. By adjusting VR3 the output can be adjusted to exactly zero before a load is applied to the member being tested.

In practice, strain gauges tend to be used in pairs or groups, often measuring the strain in various parts of a structure at the same
35 time. When used like this they are often linked to a computer rather than a series of display meters. The computer keeps a constant check on the outputs from each of the strain gauges, making sure that no part of the structure is being loaded beyond normal limits.

Source: P. Fowler and M. Horsley, 'Control Systems in the Home', *CDT: Technology*

17 Portable generator

Tuning-in

Task 1

List the different ways in which electricity can be generated.

Reading *Reading diagrams*

Task 2

Study the diagram below of a portable generator. Answer these questions using the diagram and your own knowledge of engineering.

1 What are its main parts?
2 What does the engine run on?
3 What are the four strokes called?
4 What is the function of the crankshaft?
5 What do both stator and rotor have?
6 What is the difference between stator and rotor?

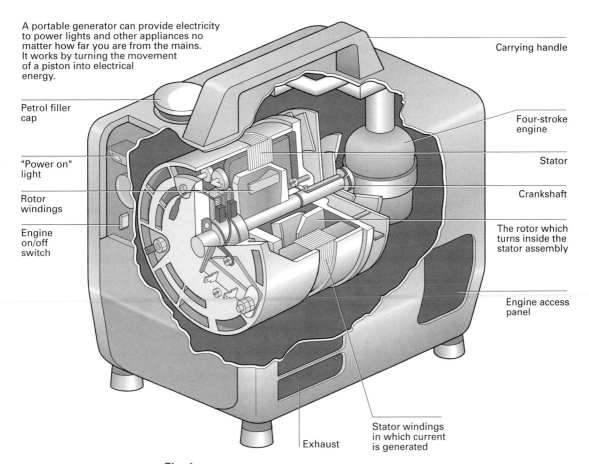

A portable generator can provide electricity to power lights and other appliances no matter how far you are from the mains. It works by turning the movement of a piston into electrical energy.

Petrol filler cap

"Power on" light

Rotor windings

Engine on/off switch

Carrying handle

Four-stroke engine

Stator

Crankshaft

The rotor which turns inside the stator assembly

Engine access panel

Exhaust

Stator windings in which current is generated

Fig. 1

Task 3   Read this text to check as many of the answers as you can. You will not find complete answers to all of the questions.

Portable generator

Although most electricity comes from power stations, power can also be generated by far smaller means. Nowadays, electricity generators can be small enough to hold in the hand.

Portable generators are made up of two main parts: an engine,
5 which powers the equipment, and an alternator, which converts motion into electricity.

The engine shown (Fig. 1) runs on petrol. It is started by pulling a cord. This creates a spark inside which ignites the fuel mixture.

In a typical four-stroke engine, when the piston descends, the air
10 inlet valve opens and a mixture of air and petrol is sucked in through a carburettor.

The valve closes, the piston rises on the compression stroke and a spark within the upper chamber ignites the mixture. This mini-explosion pushes the piston back down, and as it rises again the
15 fumes formed by the ignition are forced out through the exhaust valve.

This cycle is repeated many times per second. The moving piston makes the crankshaft rotate at great speed.

The crankshaft extends directly to an alternator, which consists of
20 two main sets of windings – coils of insulated copper wire wound closely around an iron core. One set, called stator windings, is in a fixed position and shaped like a broad ring. The other set, the armature windings, is wound on the rotor which is fixed to the rotating crankshaft. The rotor makes about 3,000 revolutions per
25 minute.

The rotor is magnetized and as it spins round, electricity is generated in the stator windings through the process of electromagnetic induction. The electric current is fed to the output terminals or sockets.

30 This type of generator can produce a 700 watt output, enough to operate lights, television, and some domestic appliances. Larger versions provide emergency power to hospitals and factories.

Source: Adapted from 'Inside out: Portable generator', *Education Guardian*

Task 4   Study this text on the four-stroke cycle. Then label each stroke correctly in Fig. 2 opposite.

In the four-stroke cycle, the piston descends on the intake stroke, during which the inlet valve is open. The piston ascends on the compression stroke with both valves closed and ignition takes place at the top of the stroke. The power or expansion stroke
5 follows. The gas generated by the burning fuel expands rapidly, driving the piston down, both valves remaining closed. The cycle is completed by the exhaust stroke, as the piston ascends once more, forcing the products of combustion out through the exhaust valve. The cycle then repeats itself.

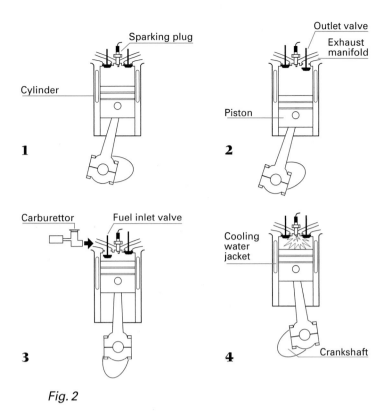

Fig. 2

Language study *Cause and effect, 2*

Study these pairs of actions. What is the link between each pair?

1 The gas expands.

2 This drives the piston down.

3 The piston ascends.

4 This forces the products of combustion out.

There are two links between the actions:

They happen at the same time. We can show this using *As* (see Unit 8).

1+2 **As** *the gas expands, it drives the piston down.*
3+4 **As** *the piston ascends, it forces the products of combustion out.*

One is a cause and the other an effect.

1 Cause: The gas expands.

2 Effect: This drives the piston down.

3 Cause: The piston ascends.

4 Effect: This forces the products of combustion out.

We can show both the time link and the cause and effect link like this:

1+2 *The gas expands,* **driving** *the piston down.*
3+4 *The piston ascends,* **forcing** *the products of combustion out.*

	Task 5	Link these actions in the same way.

Task 5 Link these actions in the same way.

	Cause	**Effect**
1	The piston moves down the cylinder.	This creates a partial vacuum.
2	The piston creates a vacuum.	This draws in fuel from the carburettor.
3	The piston moves up the cylinder.	This compresses the mixture.
4	The gas expands quickly.	This pushes the piston down.
5	The piston moves up and down.	This rotates the crankshaft.
6	The crankshaft spins round.	This turns the rotor at 3,000 rpm.
7	The armature of the alternator rotates.	This induces a current in the stator windings.
8	The alternator runs at a steady 3,000 rpm.	This generates around 700 watts.

Word study *Verbs with -ize/-ise*

Study this statement:

> *The rotor is **magnetized**.*

What does it mean? Can you say it another way? We can rewrite this statement as:

> *The rotor is **made magnetic**.*

Verbs ending in *-ize/-ise* have a range of meanings with the general sense of *make* + adjective.

Task 6 Rewrite these sentences replacing the phrases in italics with appropriate *-ize/-ise* verbs.

1. Some cars are fitted with a security device which *makes* the engine *immobile*.
2. In areas where the power supply fluctuates, for sensitive equipment a device to *make* the voltage *stable* is required.
3. Manufacturers seek to *keep* costs *to a minimum* and profits *to a maximum*.
4. Most companies have *installed computers to control* their production line.
5. Companies may *make* their operation *more rational* by reducing the variety of products they make.

Writing *Describing a process, 3: sequence and location*

Task 7 Fig. 3 opposite shows the distribution of power from power station to consumer. The statements which follow describe the distribution. Put the statements in the correct order with the help of the diagram. The first one has been done for you.

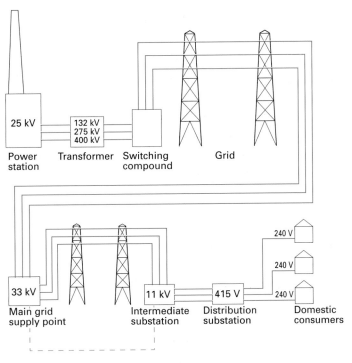

Fig. 3

a It is fed to distribution substations. ⎯⎯

b It is stepped up by a transformer to high voltages for long-distance distribution. ⎯⎯

c It is distributed via the grid to supply points. ⎯⎯

d It is distributed to the domestic consumer. ⎯⎯

e Electricity is generated at the power station at 25 kV. *1*

f It passes via the switching compound to the grid. ⎯⎯

g It is distributed via overhead or underground cables to intermediate substations. ⎯⎯

Task 8   Mark the sequence of stages using appropriate sequence words where you think this is helpful. Add the following information to your statements and make them into a text.

1 At the main grid supply points, power is stepped down to 33 kV for distribution to heavy industry.

2 At intermediate substations, power is reduced to 11 kV for light industry.

3 At the distribution substations, power is stepped down to 415 V, 3-phase, and 240 V, 1-phase.

Task 9

The two texts which follow describe two plants for generating electricity from wave power. Note the similarities and differences between the plants.

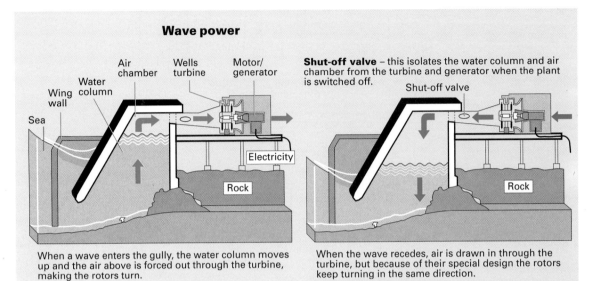

Wave power

When a wave enters the gully, the water column moves up and the air above is forced out through the turbine, making the rotors turn.

Shut-off valve – this isolates the water column and air chamber from the turbine and generator when the plant is switched off.

When the wave recedes, air is drawn in through the turbine, but because of their special design the rotors keep turning in the same direction.

Fig. 4

This prototype wave-power plant on the Scottish island of Islay was constructed by building a concrete water column across a natural gully on the shoreline. Waves flowing in and out of the gully cause water in the column to move up and down. As the water moves up
5   it compresses the air above and forces it through a wide tube at the back of the water column. As the water moves down, air is drawn into the water column.

The moving air passes through a turbine coupled to a generator. Both the turbine and generator are unusual. The turbine is a Wells
10 turbine (named after its inventor) which keeps turning in one direction even though the air flow is constantly changing direction. It has two rotors, each with four blades.

The generator is a wound rotor induction motor, which acts as a generator when it is turning at speeds greater than 1,500 rpm.
15 Below that speed it operates as a motor and takes power from the grid. This motor/generator is used because the turbine takes some time to build up to a speed where it can generate electricity. When the turbine slows down due to a lull in wave activity, the generator becomes an electric motor and keeps the turbine running at a
20 minimum speed so that it is ready to accept the power from the next batch of waves.

The plant is controlled by a computer. It includes a PLC (programmable logic controller), which monitors the operation of the motor/generator and the amount of electricity going to or being

▶

taken from the grid. There is also testing equipment to monitor how much electricity the plant is producing and the efficiency of the water column, turbine, and generator.

This experimental plant generates 150 kW. Plans have been approved for the construction of a 1 MW scheme.

Source: Adapted from 'Inside out: Wave power', *Education Guardian*

High hopes for wave power project

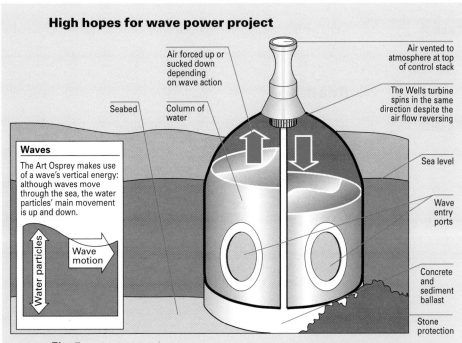

Air forced up or sucked down depending on wave action

Air vented to atmosphere at top of control stack

Seabed

Column of water

The Wells turbine spins in the same direction despite the air flow reversing

Waves

The Art Osprey makes use of a wave's vertical energy: although waves move through the sea, the water particles' main movement is up and down.

Water particles

Wave motion

Sea level

Wave entry ports

Concrete and sediment ballast

Stone protection

Fig. 5

The world's first power station in the open sea is to be stationed off Dounreay in Scotland. The machine, called Osprey (Ocean Swell-Powered Renewable Energy), will stand in 18 metres of water a kilometre out and not only harvest the larger waves, which produce
5 higher outputs, but also gain power with waves from any direction.

The device is known as an oscillating water column. As a wave rises, air is pushed through an air turbine and sucked back again as the wave falls. The turbine has been designed by Professor Alan Wells, of Queen's University, Belfast. It will generate 2 megawatts.

10 There is potential for 300 Ospreys in Scottish waters which could provide 10 per cent of the country's peak electricity demand.

18 Road breaker

Task 1 In your group, make a list of any devices you know which use compressed air.

Task 2 List any advantages compressed-air devices have compared with electrical devices.

Reading

Task 3 Read the text below and the diagram opposite to check your answers to Tasks 1 and 2.

Road breaker

Air has considerable power when it is compressed. Compressed air is used to drive all sorts of machines, from construction tools to paint sprayers.

Pneumatic or air-driven machines all make use of the force exerted
5 by air molecules striking a surface. Compressed air exerts a greater pressure than the air on the other side of the surface, which is at atmospheric pressure. The difference in pressure drives the machine.

Pneumatic drills, or road breakers, are powered by compressed air
10 produced by a compressor. Compressed-air power is cheap and safe. An air device does not risk creating sparks in an explosive atmosphere and can be used under wet conditions without danger of electric shocks. Compressed air is therefore the only type of power used in some mining or construction operations.

15 A pneumatic drill works a little like an automatic hammer. The compressor pumps the compressed air to the drill through a hose. There it drives a piston up and down. The movement of the piston delivers repeated blows to the chisel that hammers into the road surface.

20 Pressing the throttle, or control lever, downwards releases the control valve. This allows compressed air to enter the drill. The air passes through the valve and down a chamber called a return chamber to the underside of the piston. The pressure forces the piston to rise up the cylinder. As the piston rises, it covers the
25 exhaust, preventing the air from escaping. At the same time, the rising piston starts to compress the air trapped above it.

▶

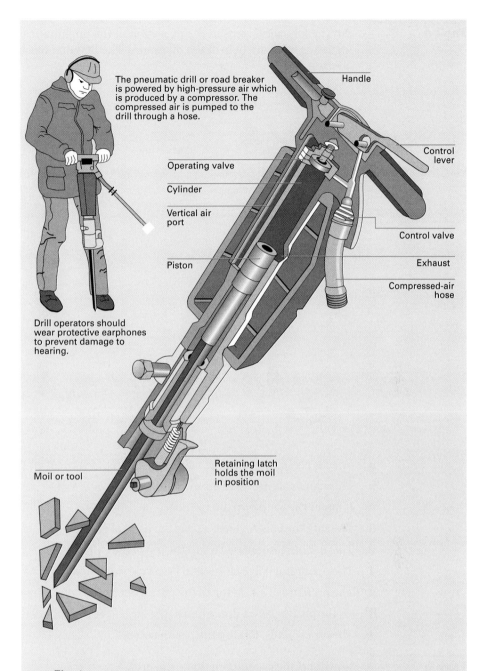

The pneumatic drill or road breaker is powered by high-pressure air which is produced by a compressor. The compressed air is pumped to the drill through a hose.

Handle

Operating valve

Cylinder

Vertical air port

Piston

Control lever

Control valve

Exhaust

Compressed-air hose

Drill operators should wear protective earphones to prevent damage to hearing.

Moil or tool

Retaining latch holds the moil in position

Fig. 1

The increase in pressure forces the operating valve to open, admitting air to the top of the chamber and closing off air in the return chamber. As the pressure in the chamber increases to 620 kPa (90 psi), it forces the piston to strike the chisel. When the piston passes the exhaust, the air is released into the atmosphere and the valve closes. This opens the return chamber again, which allows the air to pass to the underside of the piston and restarts the cycle.

30

Source: 'Inside out: Road breaker', *Education Guardian*

Put the following steps in the operation of the pneumatic drill in the correct sequence with the help of the diagrams. The first one has been done for you as an example.

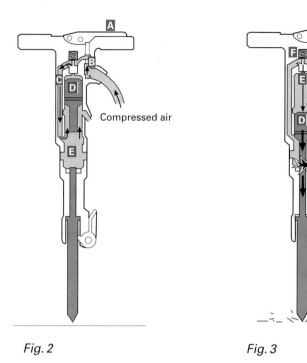

Fig. 2   Fig. 3

a The air passes through the valve and down the vertical air port. _____

b This allows compressed air into the drill. _____

c It forces the piston up the cylinder. _____

d Pressing the control lever opens the control valve. *1*

e This admits compressed air to the top of the cylinder. _____

f The operating valve closes and the cycle starts again. _____

g The pressure of air on top of the piston opens the operating valve. _____

h As the piston passes the exhaust, the air leaves the cylinder. _____

i The air expands, forcing the piston down. _____

Task 5

Now label these components of the drill.

A _____

B _____

C _____

D _____

E _____

F _____

G _____

Language study *Allow* and ***prevent*** links

Task 6

Fig. 4 shows the most basic components of a pneumatic system, a three-port valve (3PV) and a single acting cylinder (SAC). The steps below describe the operation of the system when the push button of the valve is pressed. The first step is **a**. Put the others in the correct sequence.

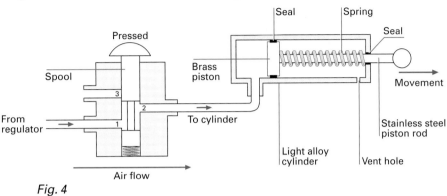

Fig. 4

a   The push button is pressed.   *1*

b   Port 3 is blocked.   _____

c   Ports 1 and 2 are connected.   _____

d   The piston compresses the spring.   _____

e   The spool is pushed down.   _____

f   Air cannot escape.   _____

g   Compressed air flows through the valve to the SAC.   _____

h   The compressed air pushes the piston along.   _____

Study these steps from the operation of the valve.

    3   Ports 1 and 2 are connected.

    4   Compressed air flows through the valve to the SAC.

    5   Port 3 is blocked.

    6   Air cannot escape.

What is the connection between Step 3 and Step 4?
What is the connection between Step 5 and Step 6?

Step 3 *allows* Step 4 to happen. We can link the steps in three ways like this:

    a   *Ports 1 and 2 are connected. This **allows** compressed air **to** flow through the valve to the SAC.*

    b   *Ports 1 and 2 are connected. This **permits** compressed air **to** flow through the valve to the SAC.*

    c   *Ports 1 and 2 are connected. This **lets** compressed air flow through the valve to the SAC.*

Step 5 *prevents* something. We can link steps 5 and 6 like this:

    *Port 3 is blocked. This **prevents** air **from** escaping.*

Complete the blanks in this description of the operation of the valve with the button pressed.

[1]_____ the push button is pressed, the spool is pushed down,

[2]_____ ports 1 and 2. This [3]_____ compressed air to flow through

the valve to the SAC. Port 3 is blocked, which[4]_____ air from escaping.

The compressed air pushes the piston along, [5]_____ the spring.

Task 8

Fig. 5 shows the system with the push button of the valve released.

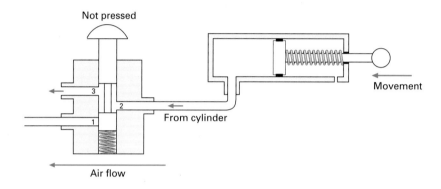

Fig. 5

These are the steps in the operation. Fill in the blanks in the steps.

a   The push button is released.

b   The valve spring [1]_____ up the spool.

c   Ports 2 and 3 are [2]_____.

d   Air from the SAC escapes through [3]_____.

e   Port 1 is [4]_____.

f   Compressed air cannot enter the [5]_____.

g   The cylinder spring pushes the [6]_____ back in.

Task 9

Now write your own description of how the system operates when the push button is released.

Writing *Explaining an operation*

Task 10

These steps explain the operation of a road breaker. Link each set of steps into a sentence using the words or phrases provided. Omit unnecessary words and make any other changes required.

1 *Pressing ... allowing*
   Press the control lever.
   This opens the control valve.
   This allows compressed air to enter the drill.

2 *... forcing ...*
   The air passes through the valve and down the return chamber to the underside of the piston.
   The pressure forces the piston to rise up the cylinder.

3 *As ... which*
   The piston rises.
   The piston covers the exhaust.
   This prevents the air from escaping.

4 *At the same time ... which*
   The rising piston starts to compress the air.
   The air is trapped above it.

5 *... admitting ... and closing ...*
   The increase in pressure forces the operating valve to open.
   This admits air to the top of the chamber.
   This closes off air in the return chamber.

6 *As ...*
   The pressure in the chamber increases to 620 kPa.
   The pressure forces the piston to strike the chisel.

7 *When ... and ...*
   The piston passes the exhaust.
   The air is released into the atmosphere.
   The valve closes.

8 *... which ... and ...*
   This opens the return chamber again.
   This allows the air to pass to the underside of the piston.
   This restarts the cycle.

Technical reading *Air skates*

Task 11

Skim the following extract from a company's sales literature to identify the paragraphs which describe:

a what an air skate consists of
b the advantages of air skates
c the differences between systems
d sizes, loads, and lift height
e air pressure required

AIR FILM MATERIAL HANDLING SYSTEMS

para
1 Material handling systems using the air film principle are also known as Air Skates.

2 The handling of light to very heavy objects using air film to float the load is easy and very economical. A weight of 1,000 kg requires a pulling force of only 1 kg.

3 An air film skate is composed of a supporting backplate with an O-shaped flexible cushion or element which is inflated by means of compressed air. The escaping air forms a thin film (approx. 0.02 mm) between the element and floor.

4 Three or more air skates combine to ensure that the load starts floating and has the ability for omni-directional movement. The load to be moved is lifted only a few centimetres and as a result of the low pressure (1–2 bar) no clouds of dust are formed and the floor cannot be damaged.

5 The dimensions of the air skates are very small. Four skates of 30 cm x 30 cm can lift 2,000 kg. The lift height is approx. 1.5 cm. Four skates of 50 x 50 cm can lift 10,000 kg. The lift height is 1.5 cm. Combinations of air skates providing a lift capacity up to 100 tonnes are not exceptional.

6 When an object is moved using an air film system, a regulator unit correctly distributes the compressed air to the air skates and can compensate for out-of-balance loads. In this way the load is lifted vertically and the load can be moved effortlessly and positioned accurately.

7 The air skates operate on air volume supplied by a compressor or pneumatic supply system working at a pressure of 5–10 bar (500–1000 kPa).

8 The air skates may be placed separately under the load which is easily accomplished due to the low height. Two basic systems are available, each with its own characteristics. The external differences in operation of the two systems are shown in the diagrams below.

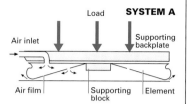

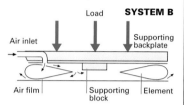

9 The specific application for each customer determines the choice of the system, the operating pressure, the element material, etc. Hence, it is necessary to obtain accurate details to get optimal effect from the system.

10 The use of air film handling techniques is not always considered. Customers who have used the method have been amply rewarded with the following advantages:

– Very efficient
– Limited investment
– Reliable
– Minimal maintenance
– Ergonomic
– Can be used with equal success indoors and outdoors
– Long working life
– Quickly fitted

Source: 'Why not let your handling problems float away on air?' Aerofilms Systems b.v.

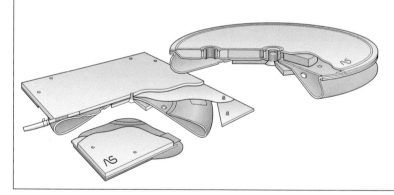

Task 12

Scan the extract to find the answers to these questions.

1 How many skates do you need to lift two tonnes?
2 What pressure of air must the compressor supply?
3 What depth is the air film between skate and floor?
4 What force is required to pull a load of one tonne?
5 Can the system be used outdoors?
6 How high, typically, is the load lifted?
7 What does the regulator unit do?
8 How is the air film formed?

Speaking practice

Task 13

Work in pairs, **A** and **B**. You each have a diagram to illustrate the symbols of the International Standards Organisation for pneumatic components. Not all of the symbols are labelled in your diagrams. Your task is to complete the labelling of your diagrams with the help of your partner.

Remember, you must not show your diagrams to each other.

Student A: Your diagram is on page 179.
Student B: Your diagram is on page 183.

19 Disc brakes

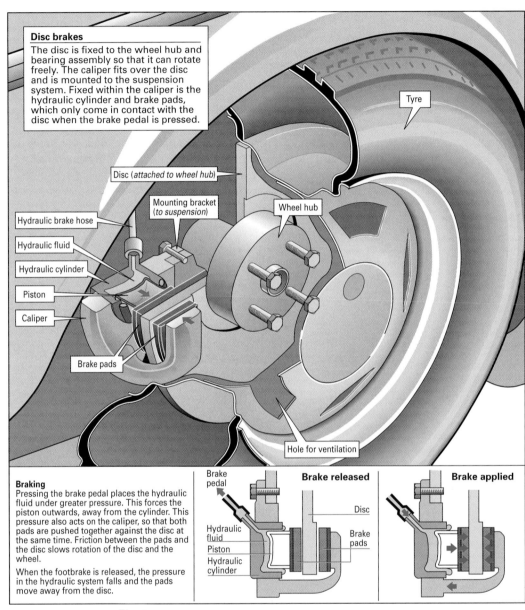

Disc brakes
The disc is fixed to the wheel hub and bearing assembly so that it can rotate freely. The caliper fits over the disc and is mounted to the suspension system. Fixed within the caliper is the hydraulic cylinder and brake pads, which only come in contact with the disc when the brake pedal is pressed.

Tyre

Disc (*attached to wheel hub*)

Mounting bracket (*to suspension*)

Wheel hub

Hydraulic brake hose

Hydraulic fluid

Hydraulic cylinder

Piston

Caliper

Brake pads

Hole for ventilation

Braking
Pressing the brake pedal places the hydraulic fluid under greater pressure. This forces the piston outwards, away from the cylinder. This pressure also acts on the caliper, so that both pads are pushed together against the disc at the same time. Friction between the pads and the disc slows rotation of the disc and the wheel.

When the footbrake is released, the pressure in the hydraulic system falls and the pads move away from the disc.

Brake pedal

Brake released

Disc

Hydraulic fluid

Piston

Hydraulic cylinder

Brake pads

Brake applied

Fig. 1

Tuning-in

Task 1

Discuss these questions in your group.

1 What forms of transport use brakes?
2 What different kinds of brakes are there?
3 How do car brakes operate?

Reading *Combining skills*

Although we have examined the skills separately, in practice we use a mix of skills when we read, depending on our purpose and the level of the text. In the tasks which follow, we will practise skimming, predicting, and scanning.

Task 2

Study the diagram on page 106 to get a general idea of what the text in Task 5 below contains.

Task 3

Skim the text below to find which paragraphs contain information on these aspects of disc brakes.

Information	Paragraph
a The hydraulics of braking	____
b Principles on which disc brakes operate	____
c The operation of the caliper system	____
d Consequences of heat generated in braking	____
e Energy conversion in braking	____

Task 4

Using your answers to Task 3, predict which paragraphs will have the answers to these questions.

   a What is the function of the calipers?
   b Why do car wheels have vent holes?
   c Where are the brakes mounted?
   d What type of material are brake pads made from?
   e What is the difference between the master and the wheel cylinder?
   f What kind of energy does a moving vehicle have?

Task 5

Scan the text to check your predictions in Task 4, and find the answers to the questions.

Disc brakes

para

Disc brakes are used on cars and motorcycles. They work by using friction and hydraulic power. The friction is generated when the brakes – stationary pads mounted to the suspension system – rub against metal discs turning with the wheels. ... *1*

5 The pads are covered with a high-friction material. The resistance of the pads against the rotating discs converts the energy of the moving vehicle (kinetic energy) into heat energy in the brakes. As kinetic energy is lost, the car slows down. ... *2*

This method of braking produces a great deal of heat, so brakes 10 have to be made from a heat-resistant material, like asbestos. The intense heat also explains why car wheels need vent-holes around the centre: when the car is moving the slots ensure a flow of air over the brakes, helping to cool them down. ... *3*

When the driver presses the brake pedal, it pushes down the 15 piston in the master cylinder, so creating pressure in the fluid. The fluid is incompressible. The pressure is transmitted to the wheel cylinder which forces the brake pads against the revolving disc. The master cylinder has a smaller diameter than the wheel cylinder. ▶ ... *4*

Hence, a relatively small force applied on the pedal produces a
20 large force on the brake pads.

The brake pads are held in a clamping device called a caliper.   5
The caliper system ensures that one brake pad is pushed against
the inner surface of the disc while, simultaneously, the other pad is
pulled against the outer surface. This gives twice the braking
25 power. The action is like squeezing something between forefinger
and thumb.

Source: Adapted from 'Inside out: Disc brakes', *Education Guardian*

Language study *Verbs with* **up** *and* **down**

In this book, you have studied a number of verbs followed by *up* or *down*. For
example:

1 *Transformers step* **up** *the voltage from 25 kV to 400 kV for transmission.*
2 *Use as little force as possible to break* **down** *a machine into its components.*

Task 6

Fill in the blanks in these sentences with either *up* or *down*. You have studied
these verbs in similar contexts.

1 As the car slows _____, kinetic energy is converted to heat.

2 An installation technician connects _____ cables and switchgear.

3 A plastic pellet in a washing machine door heats _____ and pushes the lock
into position.

4 Car wheels are ventilated to cool _____ the brake discs.

5 Transformers are used on construction sites to step _____ the mains voltage
to avoid accidents with hand tools.

6 Students in David's maths class were split _____ into three groups.

7 One of Lucy's friends came _____ with the name Swingex-L.

8 Students should keep _____ with subjects like maths and physics.

Word study *Verbs + -en*

Can you rewrite this sentence replacing the verb in italics with another verb or
phrase of similar meaning?

The caliper system *ensures* that the disc is gripped on both sides.

Here is one way it can be done.

The caliper system **makes sure** *that the disc is gripped on both sides.*

Verbs beginning or ending with *en* often have the meaning of *become/make +
adjective*.

Task 7

Replace the words in italics in the following sentences with a suitable *en* verb
from this list.

ensure	enlarge	harden	lengthen	lessen	lighten
loosen	roughen	sharpen	shorten	soften	strengthen
tighten	toughen	weaken	widen		

1 Steel rods are used to *make* concrete beams *stronger*.
2 A torque wrench is used to *make* cylinder head bolts *tight*.
3 Thermoplastics can be *made soft* by heating them.
4 After thermosetting plastics *become hard*, they cannot be softened again.
5 A reamer is a tool used to *make* a hole *larger*.
6 Corrosion *makes* structures *weak*.
7 Compressive forces will *make* a beam *shorter*; tensile forces will *make* it *longer*.
8 Carbon fibre frames *make* racing bicycles *lighter* and *stronger*.
9 Oil can be used to *make* tight bolts *loose*.
10 Carbon steels are *made tough* by heating and quenching.

Writing *Explaining an operation*

Task 8

Link the statements below to explain the operation of a hydraulic jack. Use the diagram to help you.

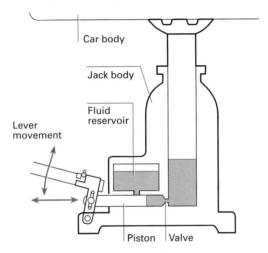

Fig. 2

1 The jack is placed under the car.
  The lever is moved up and down.
2 The movement is converted into a reciprocating motion.
  The motion slides the piston back and forwards.
3 Each movement of the piston pumps a small amount of fluid.
  The fluid is pumped from the reservoir through the one-way valve into the main cylinder.
4 This action gradually raises the jack.
  The car is lifted from the ground.
5 The car is lowered.
  This is done by releasing the one-way valve.
6 This allows the weight of the car to force fluid from the cylinder back into the reservoir.
  The car slowly descends.

Task 9

Divide your explanation into two paragraphs. Include a reference to Fig. 2.

Technical reading *Water-based hydraulics*

Task 10

Find the answers to these questions in the text which follows.

1 Why is oil superior to water as a hydraulic fluid?
2 Why were water-containing fluids developed?
3 How can the wear of metal parts be reduced in water-based hydraulic equipment?
4 What materials should be used where possible for component surfaces in sliding contact?
5 Why is sealing difficult with water-containing fluids?
6 Why is filtration of sea-water advised?

Hydraulic power was first based on water. The development of the oil industry meant the ready availability of power transmission fluids with improved characteristics compared to water. Oil has better lubrication ability and increased viscosity which allowed
5 much higher contact loads to be achieved in the machinery as well as lower leakage rates.

Water-containing hydraulic fluids have evolved since the late 1940s in response to the fire ignition risks of oil systems. The safety concerns of the steel, mining, and offshore users have played a
10 major part here.

Initially, these fluids were 40/60 water/oil mixture but these have been progressively modified into the 95/5 systems available today. High water-based fluids have to contain additives so that internal components relying on metal upon metal contact can operate
15 without excessive wear.

▶

Water-powered machinery with its inherently non-polluting media is a very attractive prospect especially because of environmental concerns about the consequences of oil leakages and the disposal of oil residues. In order to engineer effectively for water power, the
20 following points need to be considered:

- Water lacks boundary lubrication. When oil is used as a hydraulic fluid, it provides lubrication and reduces corrosion. Machinery can operate with some rubbing contact without excessive wear. When water is used, component surfaces in
25 sliding contact should be made of corrosion-resistant non-metallic materials such as ceramics or polymers.

- Water has low viscosity. Sealing is more difficult.

- Corrosion. Metals are significantly affected by water. The use of corrosion-preventing additives or non-corrosive materials is
30 advised.

- Contamination. Using 'raw water' such as sea-water which contains significant amounts of particles and salinity can cause wear and corrosion. Filtration may be necessary.

Source: Adapted from P. Tweedale, 'Beating the fire risk with Water Based Hydraulics', *Professional Engineering*

20 Staff engineer

Tuning-in

Task 1

What do these acronyms used in engineering mean?

1 CAD
2 CAM
3 CIM
4 IT
5 MRP
6 JIT
7 PC
8 PLC

Task 2

Now read this text to check your answers.

Acronyms and concepts in engineering and process control

The IT industry's talent for reducing everything to alphabet soup is only equalled by manufacturing, which you can almost discuss without using any real words at all. But it is the only way to avoid jaw-breaking terminology like 'supervisory control and data
5 acquisition'.

CAD/CAM (Computer Aided Design/Manufacturing): Use of PCs and workstation applications to automate the design and manufacturing process. Designers use CAD/CAM to prototype designs without redrawing them by hand. Popular PC packages ▶

10 include AutoCad, VersaCad and RoboCad. Workstation systems
from IBM, DEC, HP, Intergraph, and Computervision. CAM helps in
preparation of programs to control robotic and manufacturing
equipment.

MRP (Materials Requirement Planning): Breaks down product into
15 list of components needed to build it. Helps manufacturers plan
what raw materials they need in stock.

MRP II (Manufacturing Resources Planning): Includes the concept
of MRP, but also includes aspects of order processing, distribution,
and processing time.

20 JIT (Just-in-Time Manufacturing): Carries on where MRP and MRP
II leave off. Means you only make the products you have to in order
to satisfy market needs. Process extends from design and MRP to
distribution of finished products. JIT-embracing manufacturers try
not to hold any stock, either of raw materials or finished products,
25 but make products just in time to fill customer requirements.

CAPP (Computer Aided Process Planning): Systems work out how
best to route the production of items that need to go through
several different processes.

Scada (Supervisory Control and Data Acquisition): Systems collect
30 data, monitor manufacturing processes, and produce management
reports on the effectiveness of manufacturing processes. Are often
PC systems and use graphical displays to alert shop-floor staff to
problems in a process.

Concurrent Engineering: Concept of developing different aspects
35 of a product concurrently. Products' design, manufacturing, and
documentation are integrated from the start. If design of a new
product is changed, this is automatically passed through to the
next stages of production planning. Intended to replace traditional
linear approach, where each stage has to wait for previous stage to
40 be completed. Aim is to reduce time-lag between design and
finished product.

EDM (Engineering Data Management): Part of a move towards
Concurrent Engineering and CIM (Computer Integrated
Manufacturing). Central database stores all documentation related
45 to particular products. Product manuals and technical data can be
generated from original design information, and engineers should
be able to reuse design data from previous projects. One company
has halved time between introducing a change request at the
design stage and producing complete plans.

50 PLC (Programmable Logic Control): Small, rugged controllers are
programmed via a programming panel to do a particular job in a
process. Once programmed, the controllers will do the same job as
a full computer system, but at a lower cost. They can be
reprogrammed easily to do different jobs.

Source: Adapted from J. Massey, 'On the Make', *Personal Computer Magazine*

Task 3

1 Who do you think this text was written for?
2 Some words are missing from the text—the subject of some sentences, articles (the, a, an). Why?
3 What are AutoCad, VersaCad, and RoboCad?
4 What is the difference between MRP and MRP II?
5 What do you think the advantages of JIT are?
6 What is the aim of Concurrent Engineering?

Listening

You are going to hear an interview with Edward, a staff engineer. The interview contains some of the acronyms listed in Task 1.

Task 4

Listen to the interview to find these basic facts about Edward.

1 What section does Edward lead?
2 What does his company do?
3 How long has Edward worked for the company?
4 How many people started the company?
5 What is the company's turnover?
6 Why did he become an engineer?
7 What qualification does he have?

Task 5

Fill in as many spaces as you can in this extract where Edward is describing CIM. Now listen to the interview again to check your answers and to complete any remaining gaps.

Yes. There's a ^{1}_____ database in the master ^{2}_____ in the factory. It holds specifications for every product the factory makes. Bar code ^{3}_____ read the boards coming down the production ^{4}_____ and pass the information to the ^{5}_____. The robot says, 'OK, I'm going to build product A', so it pulls the CAD ^{6}_____ from the database, and builds that product. When it's finished, it ^{7}_____ the controller and passes on to the next ^{8}_____ to be assembled.

Task 6

Answer these questions on the technical information in the interview.

1 What sort of tasks can the robots perform?
2 What are the robots driven by?
3 What do the robots use instead of PLC?

Language study *Verbs with **on** and **off***

In this book, you have studied a number of verbs followed by *on* or *off*. For example:

1   JIT **carries on** where MRP and MRP II **leave off**.
2   *When the robot has finished, it informs the controller and **passes on** to the next product.*

Task 7

Fill in the blanks in these sentences with either *on* or *off*. You have studied these verbs in similar contexts.

1   Failure means that expensive development costs must be written_____ with no result.

2   The alarm goes_____ if a window is broken.

3   When the water is hot, the control unit moves_____ to the next stage of the washing programme.

4   Components which rely_____ metal upon metal contact require lubrication.

5   A thermostat causes the gas control valve to shut_____ when the room temperature is correct.

6   Feedback is used to check_____ water level, temperature, and drum speeds.

7   A car thief would set_____ the alarm.

8   If a system is needed urgently, there is no question of knocking_____ at the usual time.

9   Power may come from a small turbine engine, running_____ a clean fuel like natural gas.

10   The accident occurred after the plane took_____ .

21 Lawn-mower

Tuning-in

Task 1 Study this diagram of a lawn-mower. Then answer the questions opposite about the diagram.

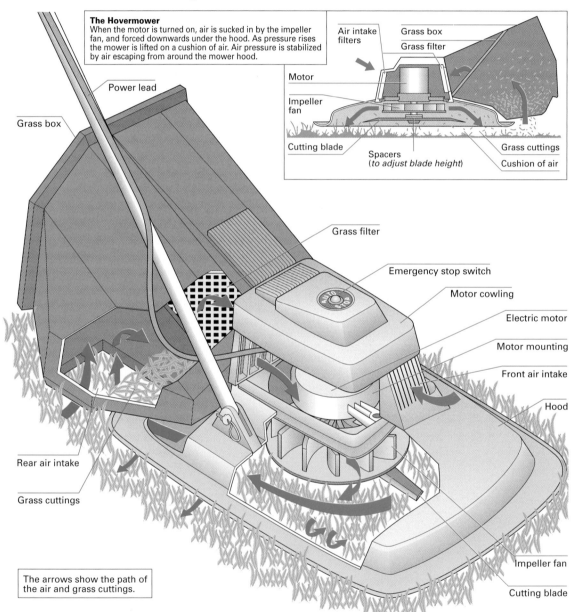

The Hovermower
When the motor is turned on, air is sucked in by the impeller fan, and forced downwards under the hood. As pressure rises the mower is lifted on a cushion of air. Air pressure is stabilized by air escaping from around the mower hood.

Air intake filters

Grass box

Grass filter

Motor

Impeller fan

Cutting blade

Spacers
(*to adjust blade height*)

Grass cuttings

Cushion of air

Power lead

Grass box

Grass filter

Emergency stop switch

Motor cowling

Electric motor

Motor mounting

Front air intake

Hood

Rear air intake

Grass cuttings

Impeller fan

Cutting blade

The arrows show the path of the air and grass cuttings.

Fig. 1

1 How is the grass cut?
2 How is the height of the cut adjusted?
3 What is the purpose of the fan?
4 How do the cuttings enter the grass box?
5 How is power provided?
6 How is the motor protected from grass intake?
7 What is the function of the hood?

Task 2 Analyse the functions of a lawn-mower by completing this 'Why and How' diagram using the labels provided below.

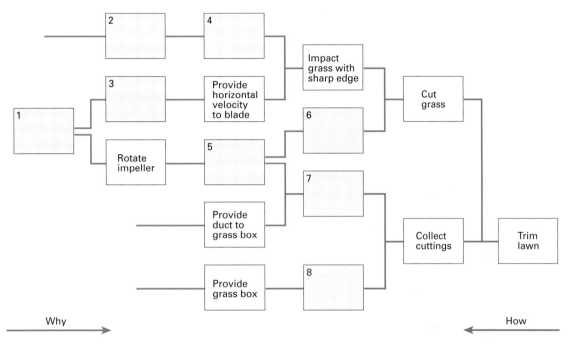

Fig. 2 *Functional Analysis System Technique (FAST) diagram*

a rotate blade
b transport cuttings
c store cuttings
d use spacers
e bring grass upright
f achieve air-flow
g provide motor
h position blade height

Reading 1 *Predicting*

You are going to read a text about engineering design. The title is:

FAST, a versatile design tool

Before you read the text, think about the answers to these questions:

1 Why do products have a finite life?
2 How can too little quality ruin a producer?
3 What does a customer require of any product?

Now read the text to check your answers and to find out the answers to these questions.

4 What is a 'window of opportunity'?
5 What is FAST?
6 What does it allow the designer to do?
7 How can a design team use FAST to put value into a design?

FAST, a versatile design tool

The task of the engineer is to produce the correct product at the correct cost at the correct time. If a product misses its window of opportunity, the manufacturer can lose up to 33% of the life cycle profits. Lost sales are never made up as changes in the market
5 place and in competitors' equipment mean that any product has a finite life.

The correct product is one which will satisfy the customer's requirements: functionality, quality, affordability, and availability. It must also satisfy the producer's requirements: low manufacturing
10 costs, simple quality control, and an identified marketing opportunity. Quality is important to both customer and manufacturer. Too much will ruin the producer, too little will alienate the customer and may also ruin the producer if faulty goods have to be recalled.

15 The designer's goal is to get it right first time. To do this a design process must be used which is effective at producing a good design. An important tool in the design process is the Functional Analysis System Technique (FAST) diagram. This enables the designer to understand the functional relationships of the system
20 being designed. The example illustrated (Fig. 2) shows the technique applied to the design of a lawn-mower.

The customer's requirement 'Trim lawn' appears in the box to the right of the diagram. Reading from the left, one can ask the question 'Why' of any of the statements contained in the other
25 boxes, and the answers will all lead to the customer's requirement. Starting from the right and asking the question 'How' establishes the reason for the function described.

FAST has many uses – for example, to analyse a competitor's equipment. This tool also enables a design team to put value into a
30 design. The process usually involves combining a number of functions into single parts, thus reducing the number of parts and saving cost in both materials and labour.

Source: Adapted from J. Fox, 'Design tools for speed and quality', *Professional Engineering*

Reading 2 *Grammar links, 2*

Study this paragraph from the text. Some phrases have been printed in **bold.** Answer the questions in *italics* which follow them.

The designer's goal is to get it right first time. To **do this** [*To do what?*] a design process must be used which is effective at producing a good design. An important tool in the design process is the Functional Analysis System Technique (FAST) diagram. **This** [*What?*] enables the designer to understand the functional relationships of the system being designed. The example shows **the technique** [*Which technique?*] applied to the design of a lawn mower.

In Units 5 and 9 we studied how texts are held together by grammar links and meaning links. The text above contains some common grammar links. Such links may cause problems for the reader who reads sentence by sentence because words seem to disappear or change. For example:

1 To **do this** *a design process must be used* means
   To ***get it right first time***, *a design process must be used*

2 ***This*** *enables the designer to understand* means
   The FAST diagram *enables the designer to understand*

3 *The example shows **the technique** applied to the design of a lawn-mower* means
   *The example shows **the Functional Analysis System Technique** applied to the design of a lawn-mower.*

Task 4

This text has more examples of the links studied here and in earlier units. Answer the questions in the text.

On most mowers, a motor with a power of around 1 kW is used to drive the cutter and fan at over 6,000 revolutions per minute (about the same [*Same what?*] as a fast-revving car). The motor is usually electric but some types [*Of what?*] use petrol engines. The fan sucks air in through two intakes, one in front of the mower and one behind in the grass box. These currents [*Of what?*] flow past the motor, helping to keep it [*What?*] cool, before being forced under the machine. This [*What?*] supports its [*What's?*] weight.

Language study *Describing functions*

To analyse the functions of a machine, we need to be able to answer 'How' and 'Why' questions. We have studied most of these methods in previous units. We will revise them here and introduce some new methods.

1 *How questions*

Answer this question about the lawn-mower shown in Task 1.

How are the clippings stored?

We can answer 'How' questions like this:

1 With *by* + *-ing*. For example:

   *The clippings are stored **by** provid**ing** a grass box.*

2   With *used + to* verb or *used + for -ing* when the instrument is given. For example:

*A grass box is **used to store** the clippings.*
*A grass box is **used for storing** the clippings.*

2   *Why questions*

Answer this question about the lawn-mower.

Why is the impeller rotated?

We can answer 'Why' questions like this:

1   With *to* + verb

*The impeller is rotated **to achieve** air-flow.*

2   With *so that* + clause

*The impeller is rotated **so that** air-flow can be achieved.*

Task 5   Explain these functions of the lawn-mower.

1   How are the cuttings transported?
2   How is air-flow achieved?
3   How is the blade height positioned?
4   How is horizontal velocity provided to the blade?
5   How is the grass impacted with a sharp edge?
6   Why is a grass box provided?
7   Why is the grass brought upright?
8   Why are spacers used?
9   Why is air-flow achieved?
10   Why is a motor provided?

Word study *Noun + noun, 2: function*

Some noun + noun compounds in engineering contain a noun formed from a verb. You studied such nouns in Unit 15. For example:

Verb	Noun	Compound noun
exchange	*exchanger*	*heat exchanger*

Often these compounds explain the function of the object. For example:

*A heat exchanger **is used to** exchange heat.*
*A heat exchanger **is for** exchanging heat.*

Task 6   Explain the function of these objects:

1   shock absorber
2   signal generator
3   speed governor
4   battery charger
5   pressure regulator
6   circuit breaker
7   hardness tester
8   fuse holder
9   engine immobilizer
10   temperature sensor

What are the names of these objects? Check the spelling in your dictionary.

a device used to:

1 reduce the speed (of a motor)
2 indicate the level of oil (in a gear box)
3 grind the surface (of a metal plate)
4 inject fuel (into petrol or diesel engines)
5 filter oil (for an engine)
6 cut wires
7 sense moisture (in an environment)
8 count binary (numbers)
9 compress air
10 convert digital (signals) to analogue (signals)

Writing *Description and explanation*

You are going to write a description of a hovermower and an explanation of how it works.

The description will answer these questions:

1 What is the hovermower for?
2 What are its main components?
3 How are they connected?

The explanation will answer this question:

4 How does it work?

Task 8

Separate these sentences into those which describe and those which explain.

1 A hovermower is for cutting grass.
2 When the motor is turned on, air is sucked in by the impeller fan.
3 There are four main components: an electric motor, a fan, a cutting blade, and a grass box.
4 Pressure under the hood rises, which causes the mower to lift on a cushion of air.
5 Some air escapes around the hood, which stabilizes the air pressure.
6 The fan is attached to the motor.
7 The cutting blade is fixed below the fan.
8 After the blades cut the grass, the cuttings are sucked into the grass box by the flow of air to the impeller fan.
9 The whole assembly is covered by a hood.
10 The grass box is situated behind the motor.

Task 9

Form the descriptive sentences into one paragraph and the explanatory sentences into a second paragraph. Give your text a title.

Speaking practice *Explaining function*

Task 10

Work in pairs, **A** and **B**.

Student A: Use the diagram in Task 2 to ask 'How' questions of your partner like this: *How does the mower trim the lawn?* Answer any questions your partner asks with the help of the diagram.

Student B: Use the diagram in Task 2 to ask 'Why' questions of your partner like this: *Why is a grass box provided?* Answer any questions your partner asks with the help of the diagram.

22 Corrosion

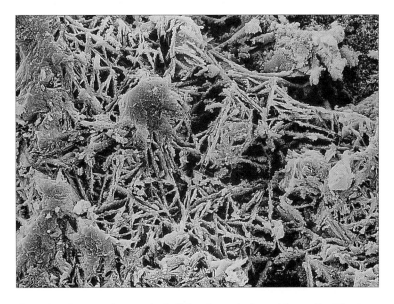

Scanning electron micrograph of a flake of rusty bodywork from a Ford Cortina car, showing a crystalline area of rust.

Tuning-in

Task 1

Study these titles of recent news items. What do you think the stories are about? Compare your predictions with other people in your group.

1 The crumbling monuments of Paris
2 Engine bolt failure blamed for air disaster

Now scan the texts to check if your predictions were correct.

The crumbling monuments of Paris

LE GRAND PALAIS, completed in 1900 and famous for shows that attract hundreds of thousands of visitors, needs £30 million in emergency restoration work. The metal frame of the palace's huge glass roof has rusted. Emergency repairs were made in the summer after iron bolts fell off but an architect's report has warned that a total collapse is possible.

An estimated £40 million is required to stop rust eating into the city's most visited monument, the futuristic Pompidou Centre, erected in 1977.

Source: Adapted from 'French art calls in the builders', *The Guardian*

Engine bolt failure blamed for air disaster

EXPERTS have confirmed that the fatal crash of a cargo plane into an apartment block was caused by failure of a bolt securing one of the plane's massive engines to the wings. Weakened by corrosion, the bolt sheared after take-off, causing one engine to break loose …

Now discuss these questions in your group:

1 What problems are caused by corrosion?
2 What if there was no corrosion?

Reading *Skimming*

Task 2

Skim the following text to identify the paragraphs which contain:

a Conditions in which corrosion occurs
b Need to consider corrosion in design
c A definition of corrosion
d Factors which limit corrosion
e Effects of rust

Corrosion

para

A major consideration in engineering design is maintenance. One   1
of the commonest causes of failure in the long term is corrosion.
This is any deterioration in the component's appearance or
physical properties.

5 Corrosion covers a number of processes whereby a metal   2
changes state as a result of some form of interaction with its
environment. It often occurs where water, either as a liquid or
vapour in air of high humidity, is present.

In general, corrosion becomes worse when impurities are   3
10 present in damp conditions. It never starts inside a material, and
there will always be surface evidence that indicates corrosion
exists, although close examination may be needed.

A common example of corrosion is the rusting of steel where a   4
conversion of metallic iron to a mixture of oxides and other
15 compounds occurs. This not only changes the appearance of the
metal but also results in a decrease in its cross-section.

It is imperative that a design takes into account whether a   5
material will be affected in a particular environment and, if
corrosion is likely, at what rate.

20 Many factors can intervene in a way to restrain its progress. An   6
example is aluminium and its alloys which perform satisfactorily in
many engineering and domestic applications when exposed to air
and water. This is due to the rapid production of a tough adherent
film of oxide which protects the metal from further attack so that
25 corrosion halts.

Source: 'Types of corrosion, how it occurs and what to look for', *Design Engineering*

Task 3

Answer these questions with the help of the text above.

1 In corrosion, why do metals change state?
2 Name two factors which encourage corrosion.
3 Where can signs of corrosion always be found?
4 What is rust?
5 Why may rust be dangerous to a structure?

6 What must designers consider regarding corrosion?

7 Why does aluminium perform well when exposed to air and water?

Language study *Cause and effect, 3*

Task 4

What connection can you see between the following?

corrosion
loss of strength
dampness
reduction in cross-section

Put them in the correct order to show this connection.

Cause and effect links like these are common in engineering explanations. You studied them first in Unit 15. You can link a cause and effect when both are nouns or noun phrases, like this:

1 If you want to put the cause first.

Cause		**Effect**
Dampness	*causes*	corrosion
	results in	
	gives rise to	
	brings about	
	leads to	

2 If you want to put the effect first.

Effect		**Cause**
Corrosion	*is caused by*	dampness
	results from	
	is the result of	
	is the effect of	
	is brought about by	
	is due to	

Task 5

Study these lists, **A** and **B**. Items in list **A** are causes of those in list **B** but the items are mixed up. Link the related items. For example:

reduction in cross-section   *loss of strength*

	A		**B**
1	reduction in cross-section	**a**	corrosion
2	insulation breakdown	**b**	bearing failure
3	overtightening	**c**	excessive heat
4	overloading a circuit	**d**	shearing in metal
5	carelessness	**e**	loss of strength
6	impurities	**f**	shearing in bolts
7	lack of lubrication	**g**	blown fuses
8	friction	**h**	short circuits
9	repeated bending	**i**	accidents
10	overrunning an electric motor	**j**	wear and tear in machinery

Now write sentences to show the link. For example:

*Loss of strength **results from** reduction in cross-section.*

Speaking practice *Exchanging information*

Task 6

Work in pairs, **A** and **B**.

Student A: Your information is on page 179.
Student B: Your information is on page 183.

Your partner has some information about two of the types of corrosion on the following list. Find out what they are and obtain information from him or her to complete as much as you can of the table below.

Types of corrosion

Common forms of corrosion are:

- general or surface corrosion
- pitting
- galvanic or bimetallic corrosion
- intergranular corrosion
- exfoliate
- demetallification
- stress corrosion
- fretting corrosion
- crevice corrosion
- microbiological corrosion

Type _____   _____

Where does it occur? _____   _____

What happens? _____   _____

What is the result? _____   _____

Technical reading *Corrosion of materials*

Task 7

Scan the table opposite to find the answers to these questions.

1   What colour is the corrosion product on nickel-base alloys?
2   Which alloys are most susceptible to pitting?
3   What does CRES refer to?
4   When is chromium susceptible to pitting?
5   What is Inconel?
6   Which alloys have the highest resistance to corrosion?
7   What is the difference in appearance between corrosion on aluminium alloys and corrosion on copper-base alloy?
8   Which CRES is more corrosion resistant?
9   What visible signs are there of corrosion in titanium alloys?
10   Name two alloys subject to intergranular corrosion.

Nature and appearance of corrosion products (Aircraft Engineering)

Alloys	Type of attack to which alloy is susceptible	Appearance of corrosion products
Aluminium alloys	Surface pitting, intergranular and exfoliation	White or grey powder
Titanium alloys	Highly corrosion resistant. Extended or repeated contact with chlorinated solvents may result in degradation of the metals' structural properties	No visible corrosion products
Magnesium alloys	Highly susceptible to pitting	White powdery snow-like mounds, and white spots on surface
Low alloy steels (4000–8000 series)	Surface oxidation and pitting, surface and intergranular	Reddish-brown oxide (rust)
Corrosion resistant steel (CRES) (300–400 series)	Intergranular corrosion (due to improper heat treatment). Some tendency to pitting in marine environment (300 series more corrosion resistant than 400 series). Stress corrosion cracking	Corrosion evidenced by rough surface; sometimes by red, brown, or black stain
Nickel-base alloys (Inconel)	Generally has good corrosion-resistant qualities. Sometimes susceptible to pitting	Green powdery deposit
Copper-base alloy, brass, bronze	Surface and intergranular corrosion	Blue or blue-green powder deposit
Chromium (used as a wear-resistant plating for steels)	Subject to pitting in chloride environments	Chromium, being cathodic to steel, does not corrode itself, but promotes rusting of steel where pits occur in the coating

Source: 'Data briefs: Corrosion of Materials', *Design Engineering*

23 Maglev train

Tuning-in

Task 1

Study this diagram of a Maglev train. What differences can you note between this and a conventional train?

Task 2

Now scan the following text quickly to check how many of the differences you have noted are mentioned. Add any other differences you find to your list.

Magnetic levitation train

A MAGLEV (magnetic levitation) train does not run along a track in the normal way. Instead, magnetic fields lift it above the track, so that the train 'floats' along.

Because they have no wheels, axles, suspension, dampers, or
5 brakes, Maglev vehicles are light and compact. They are also pollution-free, as no fuel is burned within the train, and cheap to maintain.

The Maglev system at Birmingham Airport carries passengers from the terminal to the railway station and the National Exhibition
10 Centre. The cars are made of lightweight fibreglass, carried on an aluminium chassis. ▶

All the electrical equipment which powers the cars is situated under the floors or the seats. Each car can take 32 passengers and their luggage, up to a weight of 3 tonnes. The trains travel at a maximum
15 speed of 42 km/h.

A concrete guideway above the ground supports a T-shaped track for the two-car Maglev trains. The train is lifted from the track by magnetic attraction. This is the force by which two opposite magnetic poles attract each other (just as two of the same poles
20 repel each other). Powerful electromagnets at each corner of the train exert a pulling force which lifts the train upwards so that it floats 15 mm above the track.

As people get on and off, the weight of the train varies. It may drop closer to the track than the required 15 mm, or rise further from it.
25 To keep it at an even distance from the track, the force is varied by a microprocessor.

Each train is driven by an electric motor called a linear induction motor. Electromagnetic windings, or coils, on the train generate a magnetic field in which the magnetic poles shift along the train.
30 The field induces electric current in the track, which in turn generates its own magnetic field. The two fields in the track and the train interact so that the shifting field pulls the floating train along the track.

Source: 'Inside out: Magnetic levitation train', *Education Guardian*

Reading 1 *Inferring*

Task 3

Make a list of the advantages of the Maglev train. You may use the text to help you.

Advantages

1 _____
2 _____
3 _____
4 _____
5 _____
6 _____
7 _____

Task 4

Now list the disadvantages. You may use the text to help you.

Disadvantages

1 _____
2 _____
3 _____
4 _____
5 _____
6 _____

Now think about your lists. You will probably find that most of the advantages are stated in the text. Few of the disadvantages are listed. You had to infer them, to reason them out, from your knowledge of the world and the information in the text.

Not everything we learn from a text comes from the words on the page or screen. Much of it comes from our own head. When we read, we make mental links between what we read and what we already know about the topic. In other words, we link new information and old to understand the text. This kind of reading is called *inferring*.

Reading 2 *Dealing with unfamiliar words, 2*

Answer this question using the extract from the text below.

> Why are Maglev trains so light?

> *Because they have no wheels, axles, suspension, dampers, or brakes, Maglev vehicles are light and compact.*

In your answer, you may have used the word *damper*. Do you know what it means? Do you need to know its exact meaning?

We learnt in Unit 14 that we can ignore unfamiliar words which do not help with our reading purpose. Some words we cannot ignore, but often an approximate rather than exact meaning of a word is all that is required. Sometimes we can work out the approximate meaning of a word from its context. For example, we can say that *dampers* are probably:

1 heavy (not light)

2 large (not compact)

3 part of the undercarriage (same set as wheels, axles, suspension, and brakes)

Task 5

Try to work out the approximate meaning of any of the words printed in **bold** in this text whose meaning you do not already know. Check your answers with a dictionary.

When first introduced, linear motors were seen as a major technological **breakthrough.** However, disappointingly few practical applications have been found for this new development. An earlier **innovation,** the Wankel engine, was **radically** different from conventional engines, having a rotary piston and no valves. Wankel engines were **adopted** by the Mazda car company. However, Wankel engines are now **rarely** used because of problems with fuel consumption and maintenance. The Wankel story illustrates the **risks** involved in developing any new product – success can mean a market **lead** over competitors but failure means that expensive development costs must be **written off** with no result. Sadly, technological superiority does not **guarantee** success. Betamax video tapes, technically better than their rivals, **gave way** to VHS because of better marketing.

Language study *Prediction*

Study this diagram. What will be the result of this action?

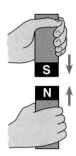

Action	**Result**
Two magnets are held together with opposite poles facing.	_____

When an action is always followed by the same result, we can link them like this:

> *If/**When** two magnets are held together with opposite poles facing, they **attract** each other.*

or

> *If/**When** two magnets are held together with opposite poles facing, they **will attract** each other.*

When an action is always followed by the same result, the statement becomes a general principle or law. (See Unit 15.) Using the law, we can predict what will happen in particular cases.

Predict the result of the action illustrated here.

Action	**Result**
Two magnets are held together with like poles facing.	_____

Now write the principle illustrated.

If two magnets _____

Task 6

Predict the results of each of these actions. Then link each action and result in a sentence.

	Action	**Result**
1	A steel bar is subjected to tensile forces.	The bar _____

F ◄—— [   ] ——► F

2 We apply an effort at E.

The block

3 The switch is closed.

4 The switch is pressed.

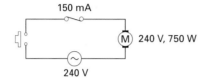

5 We move the effort by one metre.

The load

6 We move the effort by 50 centimetres.

7 The circuit is broken.

8 120 V ac is applied across the primary.

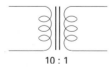

9 We apply an impact load to a brittle body.

10 We apply 24 V ac to the transformer
primary.

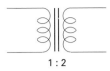

1 : 2

Writing *Explanations*

Study this diagram. It shows how a Maglev train is supported without physical contact with the track. Can you explain how this works?

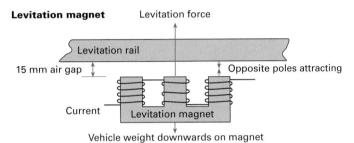

The explanation consists of a series of at least six steps. The first step is:

1 Current flows through the magnet coil.

The last step is:

6 The train is lifted.

Can you think of any of the steps in between?

Explanations consist of a series of steps. Some steps in an explanation have cause and effect links; others have time links. Here are some of the steps which explain how the train is lifted. What kinds of links are there between the stages?

1 Current flows through the magnet coil.
2 The current creates a magnetic field round the poles.
3 The field induces a current in the track.
4 The track becomes magnetized.
5 The two magnets attract each other.
6 The train is lifted.

You can show time links using the structures you studied in Unit 8. You can show cause and effect links using the structures studied in Units 16, 17, and 22, and in these ways:

> 1+2 *Current flows through the magnet coil, **creating** a magnetic field round the poles.*
>
> 3+4 *The field induces a current in the track; **therefore** the track becomes magnetized.*
>
> 5+6 *The two magnets attract each other, (**thereby**) **lifting** the train.*

Thereby can be omitted from the last example.

Task 7

Study these diagrams. They explain how the propulsion system operates.

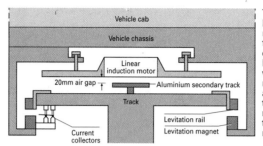

The train is propelled by a linear-induction motor mounted under the vehicle. The current creates a linear travelling field which constantly reacts with the aluminium secondary track, causing relative motion. To stop the train the current is removed.

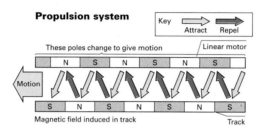

Try to complete the blanks in this set of steps which form an explanation of the propulsion system.

1 Current _____ through the motor coils.

2 The current creates _____ fields in the motor.

3 The fields _____ currents in the track.

4 The track becomes _____

5 The current through the linear motor _____ is changed.

6 The magnetic _____ in the motors shift.

7 There is _____ and repulsion between the new motor fields and the track fields.

8 The motor pulls the train along the _____ to line up the fields.

9 The _____ through the coils changes and the process is repeated.

Task 8

Divide the steps into two sets and form each set into one paragraph. Show the links between the steps using whichever method you think appropriate.

Technical reading *Motor selection: operating environment*

Task 9

What special features would you expect to see specified when rotary motors are being purchased to operate in the following situations?

1 In a workshop housing a wood planer.
2 In a boiler house which is regularly hosed down.
3 In a sewage pump house where the presence of methane gas can be expected.
4 To drive a centre lathe used for turning cast-iron components.

Read the text on the following pages to check your predictions.

When choosing a drive motor for a particular application, the following points must be considered:

1 Starting torque
2 Starting current limitation
5 3 Drive speed
4 Operating environment
5 Rating and duty cycle

We will consider here the operating environment. Attention must be given to the problem of providing sufficient cooling medium to
10 carry away the heat from the windings but at the same time not allowing that medium to carry into the motor anything which will harm it or block up the cooling ducts. Particularly harmful are oil vapour, carbon, and cast iron dust. Where machines may get wet, for example on a ship's deck, moisture ingress must be prevented
15 or suitable insulation employed.

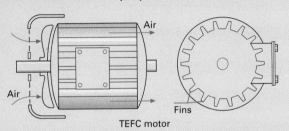

TEFC motor

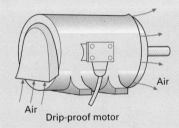

Drip-proof motor

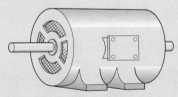

Screen protected motor protected against large solid particles

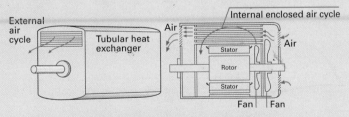

Motor with secondary cooling system protection against
most solid material and splashing water

Fig. 1

►

Probably the most commonly found machine is the totally-enclosed, fan-cooled motor (TEFC). The motor winding is totally enclosed in the motor housing which is usually ribbed on the outside. A fan is mounted on the shaft external to the housing and
20 is protected by a shield. This fan blows air over the casing removing heat from the motor. In larger sizes, there is also a fan inside the casing blowing air over the windings transferring heat to the casing.

Where motors are required to operate in explosive situations, the
25 motor must be of flame-proof construction. This means that it must be enclosed in such a manner that any explosion which may occur within the motor must be contained within the motor. Often it is easier to prevent explosive gases entering the motor. Ventilated motors are used which draw air from an uncontaminated area. This
30 is pumped into the motor which keeps its internal pressure above that of its surroundings.

Fig. 1 illustrates a variety of protected motors.

Source: Adapted from D.W. Tyler, *Electrical Applications*, 3

24 Computer Aided Design (CAD)

Tuning-in

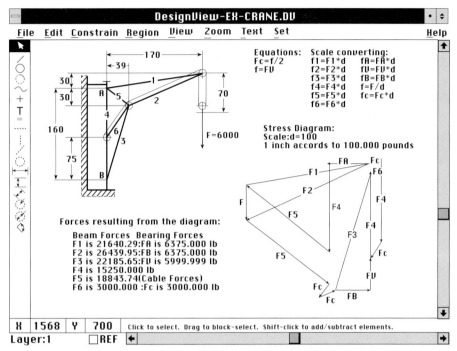

Fig. 1

Task 1

Study the example of Computer Aided Design in Fig. 1. Answer these questions about the diagram.

1 What structure does it show?
2 Apart from the design, what other information does the drawing provide?
3 What do you think the top row of words are for – File, Edit, Constrain, etc.?

Listening

Task 2

You are going to listen to an interview with a designer of car engines. He describes some of the advantages of CAD over traditional approaches to design – for example, drawing and modelling. Before you listen, list any advantages you think CAD has over these traditional approaches.

Task 3

Study the following extract from the tapescript of the interview. It covers the interviewer's first question and answer. Fill in the gaps before you listen. One word is missing from each gap. Then listen to this part of the interview to check your answers.

Interviewer: What do you like about designing on computer?

Designer: The fact that you ^{1}_____ get into three dimensions immediately. You don't ^{2}_____ to imagine how a component will ^{3}_____ from two-dimensional drawings. You can put your thoughts into the solid without ^{4}_____ to go via paper. You can see, in the mind's ^{5}_____, exactly how the components fit together or ^{6}_____ fit, and you can modify, replace, and generally tailor parts very quickly as ideas ^{7}_____ to you.

Task 4 ⊡ Now listen to the tape and list any advantages of CAD. Combine your answers with others in your group to make as full an answer as possible. When you have finished, compare your answers with the list you made in Task 2.

Task 5 ⊡ Work in pairs, **A** and **B**. Listen to the whole tape again.

Student A: Note any disadvantages of drawing in the table below.
Student B: Note any disadvantages of modelling in the table below.

Now compare notes to complete both sections of the table.

Disadvantages:

Drawing	Modelling
_____	_____
_____	_____
_____	_____
_____	_____

Task 6 The designer mentions these components of a design cycle. Put them in the correct sequence.

study results, modify design, stress analyse, design, stress analyse

---

Language study *Necessity:* **have to** *and* **need (to)**

Study these examples from the interview.

1 *You don't* **have to** *imagine how a component will look from two dimensional drawings.*
2 *... at the end of the day models* **have to** *be converted back into drawings for manufacture.*
3 *Normally one* **needs to** *go round the circle at least four times.*
4 *With CAD, you* **need** *not describe such a feature more than once.*

Have to and *need (to)* can both be used to express necessity. In this sense, they are similar to *must*. *Must* is a modal auxiliary verb and has no other forms, whereas *have to* and *need (to)* have the same range of forms as other verbs.

The table opposite shows ways of expressing necessity and no necessity in the present.

+ necessity	- necessity
have to	do not have to
need to	need not *or* do not need to
must	—

Task 7

Fill in the blanks in these sentences with appropriate forms of the verbs in the table above.

1 Designers who work with CAD _____ produce drawings on paper.

2 The production planner can use the computer model to calculate what machining _____ be done.

3 One problem in working with wood or clay models is that they _____ be converted into drawings for manufacture.

4 With traditional design, you _____ imagine a three-dimensional shape from a two-dimensional drawing.

5 With CAD, designers can put their ideas into solid shapes without _____ use paper.

6 In engineering drawing repeated features _____ be drawn again each time but with CAD they _____ be redrawn.

7 Making cars lighter _____ mean making them flimsier or less safe.

25 Supercar

Tuning-in

Task 1

Study the following recent Volkswagen survey on the car of the future. Decide in your group which developments in the survey are important to you. One person should report the group's views to the rest of the class.

What changes would you like to see?

We've suggested a few possible developments. Please think carefully about which ones would make a real difference to you and tick the boxes to let us know.

Design

☐ The opportunity to use alternative fuel sources like hybrid (petrol and diesel) or hydrogen power.

☐ A car that is an office away from work, with facilities such as a fax machine and video-conferencing.

Safety

☐ Speed limiters that vary to give you the safest possible drive for the weather and road conditions.

☐ A computer sensor to tell you if you're driving at a safe distance from the vehicle in front.

☐ Automatic engine and fuel supply cut-out in the unfortunate event of an accident.

☐ All-round airbags.

Security

☐ Engine immobilizer which makes it virtually impossible for anyone else to drive your car away.

☐ A tracking device which allows the car to be located fast if it is stolen.

☐ Audio systems built into the chassis or engine of the vehicle to prevent theft.

Performance

☐ Sports car performance combined with fuel economy.

☐ A computerized route finder which tells you the quickest way to get to your destination.

☐ Servicing by mobile units to save lengthy visits to a garage.

Source: V.A.G. (UK) Ltd

Task 2

What do you think will be different about cars in the next ten years? Think about the following points. Compare your ideas with other groups.

– materials
– design
– power
– fuel

Task 3

Read this title and introduction to a text. Try to guess the answers to the questions which follow.

> **Supercar test for industry**
>
> Matthew L. Wald on the technical issues the President's environmentally-friendly car faces ...

1 Who is the President?
2 Who is Matthew L. Wald?
3 How can a car be environmentally-friendly?
4 Why might a car be called a Supercar?
5 What test does industry face?

Now read the first paragraph of the text. Does it help you to answer the questions?

> The 10-year co-operative project between government and Detroit for an environmentally-correct supercar will require radically new technologies for solving the car industry's problems: air pollution, over-reliance on imported oil, and loss of market share to imports.

Reading *Predicting: using first sentences*

In earlier units we studied how reading the title and using diagrams can help you predict the contents of a text. As we saw above, reading the first paragraph can also be very helpful.

A final way to get a good idea of the contents of a text is to read the first sentence of each of the other paragraphs.

Task 4

Read these first sentences; then note down what you think the main points of the text are.

1   Some say it cannot be done but others say various components could be pulled together to do the job: electric motors with batteries, fuel cells or flywheels to deliver electricity, plus lightweight, aerodynamic car bodies.

2   Instead of steel, some other type of material would be necessary for the 'supercar' body, some kind of composite or carbon fibre.

3   Safety is another issue but lighter need not mean flimsier.

4   Reducing body weight and wind resistance will make any car more efficient.

5   Electronics can, however.

6   Four possible power sources are being investigated.

7   Another possibility is fuel cells, which combine oxygen from air with hydrogen to make electricity.

8   Yet another approach would be a flywheel, an electrical generator consisting of free-spinning wheels with magnets in the rims that can produce a current.

9   A fourth possible power source for the national supercar would be a small turbine engine, running on a clean fuel like natural gas.

Task 5

Read one of the following texts as your teacher directs: **A**, **B**, **C**, or **D**. Note in this table any information you find on solutions to the problems of designing the Supercar.

Text	Solution	Reason(s)
A **Materials**	_____	_____
B **Shape**	_____	_____
C **Power**	_____	_____
D **Power source**	**Problem**	
1 _____	_____	
2 _____	_____	
3 _____	—	
4 _____	—	

Now share your information with others in your group to complete the table.

Text A

> Some say it cannot be done but others say various components could be pulled together to do the job: electric motors with batteries, fuel cells or flywheels to deliver electricity, plus lightweight, aerodynamic car bodies. ▶

5 Instead of steel, some other type of material would be necessary for the 'supercar' body, some kind of composite or carbon fibre. Such materials are available now, but are not considered cost competitive with steel. But a research centre in Colorado claims that composites can 'emerge from the mould virtually ready to
10 use'. The result would be fewer parts and less labour than current car body construction and, therefore, less cost.

Safety is another issue but lighter need not mean flimsier. The centre points to Indy 500 drivers who routinely survive 230-mph crashes in composite vehicles.

Text B

Aerodynamic drag accounts for more and more of the energy required to move the car as speed rises. The car makers already know how to cut drag sharply. General Motors' *Impact* has about half the drag of a typical car. The *Impact* has a rounded front and a
5 tapered back. It is also small to present less frontal surface to the wind.

Text C

Reducing body weight and wind resistance will make any car more efficient. But roughly equal to the wind in eating up the car's energy is braking, and internal combustion engines cannot do much about that.

5 Electronics can, however. Nearly all electric designs use regenerative braking. When the driver hits the brake the motors become generators, converting the mechanical energy of the slowing wheels into electricity. That capability virtually guarantees that a super-efficient car will have an electric motor.

Text D

Four possible power sources are being investigated. The simple one is batteries. But if a super-efficient car is to have an attractive cruising range, it cannot carry hundreds of pounds in batteries.

Another possibility is fuel cells, which combine oxygen from air
5 with hydrogen to make electricity. But current fuel cells operate steadily, and a car cell would have to handle widely varying demand for energy: zero, while stopped at traffic lights, or several times that consumed by an average house, while accelerating.

Yet another approach would be a flywheel, an electrical generator
10 consisting of free-spinning wheels with magnets in the rims that can produce a current. An early application of flywheels might be in a race car built for a twisting course, where frequent braking means high fuel consumption in conventional cars.

A fourth possible power source for the national supercar would be
15 a small turbine engine, running on a clean fuel like natural gas. It would run at a constant speed, generating electricity for driving the vehicle or for feeding a bank of batteries, storing energy for later use.

Task 6   Read the whole text yourself. How much did the first paragraph and the first sentences of the other paragraphs help you to predict the main points of the whole text? Which first sentences were not very helpful? Why not?

Language study *Certainty*

Study these statements. What is the difference between them? Can you put them in order of certainty?

1   *A supercar **will** have an electric motor.*

2   *A supercar **might** have a flywheel.*

3   *It **is likely** that a supercar will have a rounded front.*

The difference between the statements is how certain the writer is about each development. Study this list of certainty expressions.

	Certain	**Fairly certain**	**Uncertain**
Yes	will	will probably be + likely + vb be + probable that	might may could will possibly
No	will not	be + unlikely to + vb	be possible that

Task 7

Comment on how likely these predictions are for the next decade, using an appropriate expression from the table above. For example:

1   A human powered vehicle (hpv) will exceed 100 km/h.
    It is possible that an hpv will exceed 100 km/h.

2   A perpetual motion machine will be invented.
    A perpetual motion machine will not be invented.

3   More factories will be fully automated.
    It is likely that more factories will be fully automated.

4   Driverless trains will link major cities.
    Driverless trains might link major cities.

1   Electric cars will become common.
2   Most bicycles will have carbon fibre frames.
3   A more efficient petrol engine will be developed.
4   More people will travel by public transport.
5   Robots will be used in homes.
6   Fewer engineers will be required.
7   Diesel engines will replace petrol engines for cars.
8   Most waste materials will be recycled.
9   An ideal electric motor will be invented.
10 Physicists will reach absolute zero (-273°C).

Study these statements. Why is *will* used in the first sentence and *would* in the second?

1   *A supercar **will** have an electric motor.*

2   *A possible power source **would** be a turbine engine.*

In sentence 1 the writer feels certain this will happen. In sentence 2 the writer feels this is only a possibility because it depends on circumstances.

We use *would* to describe future events which can only happen if certain conditions are met. Study these examples from the text.

Another approach *would* be a flywheel. (*If a supercar were built.*)

The result *would* be fewer parts and less labour. (*If moulded composites were used.*)

Task 8

What would happen if these conditions were met?

1 If all cars were made of plastic _____.

2 If all cars had diesel engines _____.

3 If powerful, lightweight batteries were developed _____.

4 If all cars were fitted with flywheels _____.

5 If speed limits were reduced _____.

Task 9

What conditions are necessary for these events to happen?

1 All car parts would be recyclable.
2 Cars would travel 40 km/litre of fuel.
3 Cars would cost much less to produce.
4 Cars would not require painting.
5 Cars would not require lubricants.

Writing *Summaries*

The best way to make a summary of a text is to write down the main points in note form and then link them clearly in your own words. If you are summarizing for others, make sure you do not over-summarize, that is, reduce the text to the point that no one but you can understand what it means.

Task 10

Study these notes which summarize the Supercar text.

Text		Solution	Reason(s)
A	**Materials**	composite, carbon fibre	fewer parts, less labour
B	**Shape**	rounded front, tapered back, small	reduce drag
C	**Power**	electric motor	allows regenerative braking
D	**Power source**	**Problem**	
1	batteries	weight	
2	fuel cells	cannot cope with varying demand	
3	fly wheel	—	
4	gas turbine with generator	—	

Now convert each section of the notes into one or two sentences. Use the certainty expressions you studied in this unit. For example:

> *The Supercar will have an electric motor because only electric motors allow regenerative braking.*

If you think that your reader will not understand particular terms, define them. For example:

> *The Supercar will have an electric motor because only electric motors allow regenerative braking, that is, converting braking power back into electrical energy.*

Finally, link your sentences into paragraphs. You will need at least two.

– materials, shape, and power   – possible power sources

You will also need to add a brief introductory paragraph stating the objectives of the Supercar project.

26 Graphs

Tuning-in

In engineering, graphs and charts are a common way of giving information. They allow a great deal of data to be presented easily in visual form.

Task 1

Label the following graphic displays with the correct term from this list:

graph   pie chart
bar chart   bar chart (column chart)

a

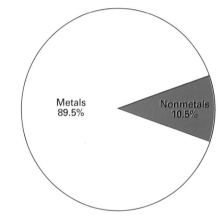

Metals
89.5%

Nonmetals
10.5%

b

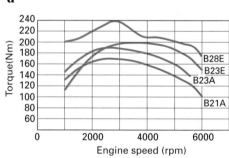

Female students as a
percentage of all students

1979/80
1989/90

Percentages

Engineering
technology

All courses

c

What goes wrong most

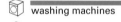
washing machines

dishwashers

colour TVs
vacuum cleaners
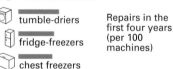
tumble-driers

fridge-freezers

chest freezers

upright freezers

Repairs in the
first four years
(per 100
machines)

d

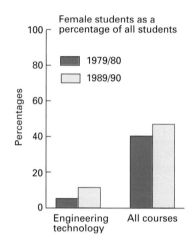

Torque(Nm)

B28E
B23E
B23A
B21A

Engine speed (rpm)

Task 2

Study the graph opposite which shows typical daily load curves for a power station. Answer these questions about the graph for weekdays.

1 When is the peak load?
2 When is there least demand?
3 When is the load 65% of capacity?
4 What is the load at 1 p.m.?

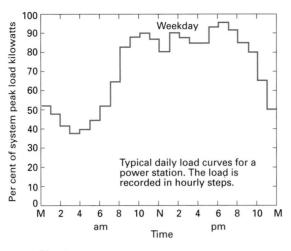

Fig. 1

Describe changes in load for these periods:

5 Between 6 a.m. and 10 a.m.
6 Between 7 p.m. and midnight.
7 Between 3 p.m. and 5 p.m.

Language study *Describing graphs*

Look at the period 6 a.m. to 10 a.m. We can describe the change in load in two ways:

1 *The load rises.*

2 *There is a rise in load.*

We can make our description more accurate like this:

3 *The load rises sharply.*

4 *There is a sharp rise in load.*

Study this table of verbs and related nouns of change. The past form of irregular verbs is given in brackets.

Direction	Verb	Noun
Up	climb	
	go up (went up)	
	increase	increase
	rise (rose)	rise
Down	decline	decline
	decrease	decrease
	dip	dip
	drop	drop
	fall (fell)	fall
	go down (went down)	
Level	not change	no change
	remain constant	

These adjectives and adverbs are used to describe the rate of change:

Adjective	Adverb
slight	slightly
gradual	gradually
steady	steadily
steep	steeply
sharp	sharply
sudden	suddenly
fast	fast

Task 3

Study this graph which shows the load at weekends.

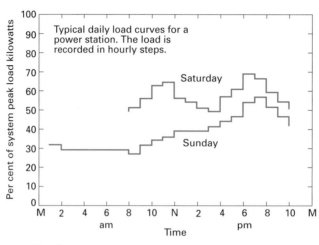

Fig. 2

Write sentences to describe the load during these periods.

1 Saturday, 8 a.m. to noon.
2 Saturday, 6 p.m. to 10 p.m.
3 Saturday, noon to 5 p.m.
4 Saturday, noon to 1 p.m.
5 Sunday, 2 a.m. to 8 a.m.
6 Sunday, 8 a.m. to 9 a.m.
7 Sunday, noon to 3 p.m.
8 Sunday, 5 p.m. to 10 p.m.

Task 4

Look at Fig. 1 and Fig. 2. Make comparisons of these periods. For example:

Sunday, 4 a.m. to 8 a.m./weekdays at the same time.

On Sunday the load remains constant between 4 a.m. and 8 a.m. but on weekdays it rises sharply.

1 Sunday, noon to 3 p.m./Saturday at the same time.
2 Weekdays, 10 p.m. to 11 p.m./Saturday at the same time.
3 Saturday peak load/Sunday peak load.
4 Sunday, noon to 1 p.m./the rest of the week at the same time.

Word study *Common verbs in engineering*

Study this list of common verbs in engineering which you have studied in this book. They all have the sense of 'make something happen'.

lower   make low
raise   make high
heat   make hot
release   make free
compress   make smaller volume
reduce   make smaller
increase   make larger

Task 5

Fill in the blanks in these sentences with suitable verbs from the list above.

1   When thermoplastics are —————— , they soften.

2   If a gas is —————— , it heats up.

3   Refrigeration preserves food by —————— its temperature.

4   A heater —————— the temperature of the water.

5   The rising piston —————— the fuel mixture.

6   Designers try to —————— the weight of a structure.

7   When the push button is —————— , the valve spring pushes up the spool.

8   Pumping fluid into the main cylinder gradually —————— the jack.

9   Aerodynamic design —————— wind resistance.

10 The motor starts up slowly, then gradually —————— speed.

11 At intermediate substations, power is —————— to 11 kV for light industry.

12 When the child —————— the handle, the seat swings back under the weight.

Writing *Describing a graph*

An important mechanical test of a metal is the tensile test to destruction. Increasing loads are applied to a specimen of the metal until it breaks. For a mild steel specimen, a graph of load against extension looks like this:

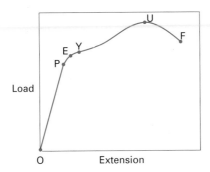

The following sentences describe the most important stages of the test. With the help of the graph:

- put the stages in the correct sequence to form a text describing the graph.
- fill in the missing references (O, P, E, Y, U, F).

a From_____ to_____ the specimen extends in direct proportion to the load applied.

b This rapid extension continues until point_____ , the maximum load, is reached.

c From_____ there is a rapid increase in length for each increase in load.

d At_____ the specimen finally fractures.

e After_____ the specimen lengthens further but the load falls.

f Soon after P the material reaches its elastic limit, marked on the graph as point

_____

Add this extra information to your text.

a Up to the elastic limit, the steel will regain its original length when the load is removed.

b Up to U there is no change in the cross-section of the steel.

c After the elastic limit, the steel will not regain its original length.

d After U the specimen undergoes 'waisting'.

e Y is the yield point.

Refer to each of these figures at an appropriate place in your text. Use expressions such as these:

As shown in Figure A.
See Figure A.
(Figure A)

A

B

C

Technical reading *Properties and applications of carbon steels*

Task 9

Study the diagram below which shows how tensile strength, hardness, and ductility vary with the percentage of carbon in carbon steels. Answer these questions:

1 What percentage of carbon gives the greatest tensile strength?
2 What happens to ductility between 0.08% and 0.87% carbon?
3 How does increased carbon affect hardness?
4 What is the effect on tensile strength of increasing carbon beyond 0.84%?
5 What happens to ductility beyond 0.87% carbon?

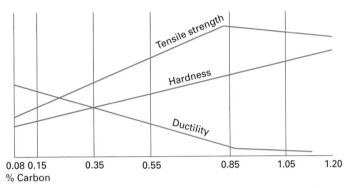

Properties of carbon steels

Task 10

Now study the diagram below for extra information and answer these questions.

1 What is high carbon steel?
2 How much carbon does tool steel contain?
3 Compare the properties of mild steel and hard steel.
4 What kind of steel is tin plate made from?
5 What kind of steel are car springs made from?

Low carbon steel	Mild steel	Medium carbon steel	High carbon steel		
			Hard steel	Spring grades	Tool steel
Tin plate, wire, rivets, pipes	Ship and boiler plates, structural sections, turbine rotors, marine shafts	Railway rails, crank pins, connecting rods, axles, gears, gun barrels	Locomotive tyres, woodcutting tools, crusher rolls, hammers, hand chisels	Car springs, tap drills, ball races	Metal cutting and forming tools, drills, wire dies

Properties and applications of carbon steels

27 Waste recycling plant

Aluminium can recycling. The bales seen here contain over one million cans.

Tuning-in

Task 1

You are going to read a text on recycling domestic refuse. The main components of refuse are given in the list below. Using your knowledge of engineering, discuss in your group how one of these components could be recovered from refuse and what use could be made of the materials recovered. Your teacher will decide which component each group will discuss.

Ferrous metals	Glass	Plastics
Paper	Organic materials	Non-ferrous metals

Task 2

Now report your solutions to the rest of the class. Be prepared to answer questions and defend your ideas.

Read the text below to see how the solutions proposed by your class compare with those used in the experimental plant described.

Recycling domestic refuse

The consumer society produces more and more refuse. A number of solutions to this problem have been proposed. In some countries refuse is burnt to generate electric power. In Germany, producers must take back unwanted packaging for recycling. In other
5   countries, householders are asked to separate out refuse so that it can be recycled more easily. This text describes an experimental plant in Holland designed to recycle domestic refuse.

The rubbish collected from households consists of a mixture of organic materials such as kitchen waste, and inorganic materials
10 such as glass and plastic bottles, tin cans, and packaging.

The rubbish is first passed through a hammer mill to shred it. The mill consists of rotating steel arms which break up any large items to reduce them to a more manageable size. Any items which may cause damage later in the process are rejected at this stage.

15 The shredded mixture passes under an electromagnet which removes ferrous metals. Much of this is tin cans. Almost all ferrous metals are recovered in this way.

After that, the residue is carried by conveyor belt to an air classifier. A stream of air is blown through the classifier, which has a zig-zag
20 shape. Low density materials such as plastic, paper, and some organic substances rise to the top of the classifier. Higher density materials such as glass and non-ferrous metals fall to the bottom and are discarded. These could be further separated out using a range of processes. For example, an eddy current mechanism
25 could screen out aluminium waste. Froth flotation techniques could recover glass.

The low density portion is carried to a rotating drum where it is screened. Fine organic materials pass through the screen leaving a mixture which consists mainly of plastic and paper. The organic
30 residue can be used for compost or to make bricks.

The next stage is to separate the plastic from the paper. This was initially a problem as both are similar in density. The solution is to wet the mixture. The paper absorbs water and as a result becomes denser than the plastic.

35 In the final stage, the wetted mixture is passed through a second air-classifier where the lighter plastic leaves from the top and the denser wet paper from the bottom. The recovered paper could be fed to pulp mills for further recycling.

The remaining plastic is a mixture of thermosets and
40 thermoplastics. It is not easy to separate these out but the mixture can be melted and formed into insulating materials for building.

Reading *Transferring information, making notes*

Task 4

Using the information in the text, complete the labelling of the flowchart. Add these labels:

plastic and paper mixture
high density materials
shredded mixture
paper
fine organic materials

air classifier
rotating drum
ferrous metals
wetted mixture

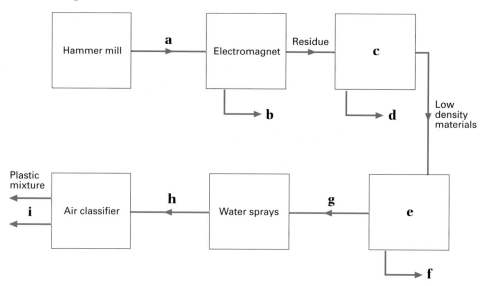

Task 5

Study these notes on the first stage of the recycling process. They contain information on location (*Where?*), action (*What happens?*), reason (*Why?*), and method (*How?*). Read the text again to complete the notes for the other stages.

Stage 1

Where?	hammer mill
What happens?	the waste is shredded
Why?	to reduce it to a manageable size
How?	using rotating steel arms to break up any large items

Stage 2

Where?	_____
What happens?	_____
How?	by magnetism

Stage 3

Where?	_____
What happens?	high and low density materials are separated
How?	by a current of air which carries low density materials to the top while high density materials fall to the bottom

Stage 4

Where?	_____
What happens?	the low density portion is screened
Why?	_____

Stage 5

What happens?	_____
Why?	to give the paper and plastic different densities

Stage 6

Where?	_____
What happens?	_____
How?	by a current of air which carries low density plastic to the top while wet paper falls to the bottom

Language study *Possibility:* **can** *and* **could**

Answer these questions about the text.

1 Does this plant screen out aluminium waste?
2 Does it recover glass?
3 Is recovered paper fed to pulp mills?
4 Is recovered plastic melted and formed into insulating blocks?
5 Is organic residue used for compost and bricks?

The answer to questions 1, 2, and 3 is *No*. The answer to questions 4 and 5 is *Yes/Maybe*. How do we know? Look at the text.

1 *An eddy current mechanism* **could** *screen out aluminium waste.*

2 *Froth flotation techniques* **could** *recover glass.*

3 *The recovered paper* **could** *be fed to pulp mills for further recycling.*

4 *The mixture* **can** *be melted and formed into insulating materials for building.*

5 *The organic residue* **can** *be used for compost or to make bricks.*

We use *could* in examples 1, 2, and 3 to show that something is possible but is not in fact done. The reasons why nothing is done in these examples may be expense or lack of demand. We do not know.

We use *can* in examples 4 and 5 to show that something is possible and may in fact be done.

Task 6

Fill in the gaps in this text with either *can* or *could*. Be prepared to justify your answers.

1 With present technology we _____ recycle almost all domestic refuse.

But in practice market forces determine what is worth recycling.

2 Successful plants in a number of countries show that refuse _____ be

used as a fuel in power stations.

3 If we recycled most of our refuse, the increasing problem of waste disposal

_____ be solved.

4 Sweaters _____ be produced from old plastic bottles. A company in the United States converts the waste plastic into polyester yarn. It takes twenty-five two-litre bottles to make a sweater.

5 At present we _____ not easily separate thermosetting plastics from thermoplastics.

Writing *Describing a process, 4: reason and method*

In Units 13 and 15 we learnt how to sequence and locate the stages in a process. In this unit we will study ways to describe and explain what happens in each stage.

Look again at the notes on Stage 1.

Stage 1

Where?	hammer mill
What happens?	the waste is shredded
Why?	to reduce it to a manageable size
How?	using rotating steel arms to break up any large items

Note how we can combine information on sequence, location, process, reason, and method. For example:

Sequence + location

> The waste **first** passes **to a hammer mill**

+ action

> The waste first passes to a hammer mill, **where it is shredded**

+ reason

> The waste first passes to a hammer mill, where it is shredded **to reduce it to a manageable size**

+ method

> The waste first passes to a hammer mill, where it is shredded to reduce it to a manageable size **using rotating steel arms** to break up any large items.

Task 7

Combine information on the other stages in the same way to make a full description of the recycling process. Note that you can help your reader understand the sequence by carrying information from one stage to the next. For example:

Stage 1   *The waste is shredded.*
Stage 2   *The **shredded waste** ...*
Stage 5   *The mixture is wetted.*
Stage 6   *The **wetted** mixture ...*

28 Robotics

Tuning-in

Task 1

Together, try to write a definition of a robot. Compare your answer with the definition of an industrial robot given on page 36 of the Answer Book.

Reading 1 *Revising skills*

In the tasks which follow, we will revise some of the reading skills you have studied.

Task 2

Study this diagram which shows the components of an industrial robot. What do you think the functions of the three components shown are?

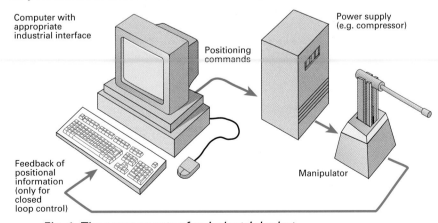

Computer with appropriate industrial interface

Positioning commands

Power supply (e.g. compressor)

Feedback of positional information (only for closed loop control)

Manipulator

Fig. 1 The components of an industrial robot

Now read this text to check your answers to Task 2.

The manipulator

This is the bit which actually does the mechanical work, and in this case it is anthropomorphic (i.e. of human-like form), resembling an arm.

The power supply

For heavy-duty hydraulic or pneumatic machines this will be a
5 compressor. In smaller, lightweight versions which use electrical stepper motors rather than hydraulics or pneumatics, this would be omitted.

The computer

The controlling computer is fitted with appropriate interfaces. These may include digital inputs, digital outputs, ADCs (analogue-
10 to-digital converters), DACs (digital-to-analogue converters), or stepper motor control ports. These control the various compressors, stepper motors, and solenoids, and receive signals from the manipulator's sensors.

Task 4

Read the following text to find the answers to these questions.

1 What is the work volume of a manipulator?
2 What is the work volume of a human?
3 Why is the work volume of a human greater than that of an industrial robot?
4 What are 'degrees of freedom'?

Work volume

Robots are multifunctional so an important design issue for the manipulator is its 'work volume': the volume of space into which it can be positioned. The greater the work volume, the more extensive the range of tasks it can be programmed to carry out.

5 As a human being, your work volume consists of all the places your hands can reach. Most industrial robots have a much more limited work volume because they are bolted to the floor. Even with the same limitation applied, however, the human body is a very flexible machine with a work volume described – very
10 approximately – by a cylinder about 2.2 m high with a radius of about 1.8 m and a domed top.

Degrees of freedom

In order to achieve flexibility of motion within a three-dimensional space, a robot manipulator needs to be able to move in at least three dimensions. The technical jargon is that it requires at least
15 three 'degrees of freedom'. Figs. 2 a–d show a number of the more common types of robot manipulator mechanisms. Each has the requisite three degrees of freedom, allowing either linear or rotational movement.

Reading 2 *Transferring information*

Study the text and accompanying diagram (Fig. 2a) below and note how the information has been transferred to Table 1.

Fig.	Type	Degrees of freedom		Work volume
		linear	rotational	
2a	Cartesian or rectilinear	3	0	cube
2b				
2c				
2d				

Table 1

Common types of manipulator

Fig. 2a is the simplest. Its three degrees of freedom are all linear and at right angles to each other, so they correspond to the three Cartesian co-ordinates. Driving it presents no mathematical difficulties, since each degree of freedom controls a single
5 Cartesian co-ordinate without affecting the others. Fairly obviously, the work volume of the Cartesian manipulator is a cube.

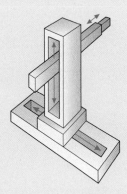

Fig. 2a Cartesian or rectilinear manipulator

Work in groups of three. Your teacher will select a text for you. Read the text and diagram to complete your section of Table 1.

Text 1

The second type of manipulator, shown in Fig. 2b, is called a cylindrical manipulator because of the shape of its work volume. It has one rotational and two linear degrees of freedom. Because of the rotational aspect, however, the maths needed to position it
5 becomes more involved, which means that for a given response speed a faster processor is necessary.

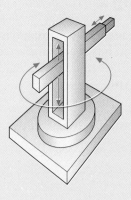

Fig. 2b Cylindrical or post-type manipulator

Text 2

Fig. 2c shows the spherical manipulator which has two rotational and one linear degrees of freedom. The work volume is indeed a sphere, and once again the complexity of positioning the device increases.

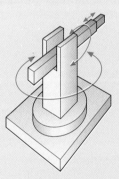

Fig. 2c Spherical or polar manipulator

Text 3

The final type of manipulator has three rotational degrees of freedom. This is the most complex type to control, but it has increased flexibility. Fig. 2d shows this type of manipulator – the anthropomorphic arm. The work volume of a practical manipulator
5 of this form is shown in Fig. 3. You will notice that it is basically spherical but has missing portions due to the presence of the arm itself and because the rotations cannot achieve a full 360 degrees. The scallops on the inner surface are caused by constraints imposed by the joints.

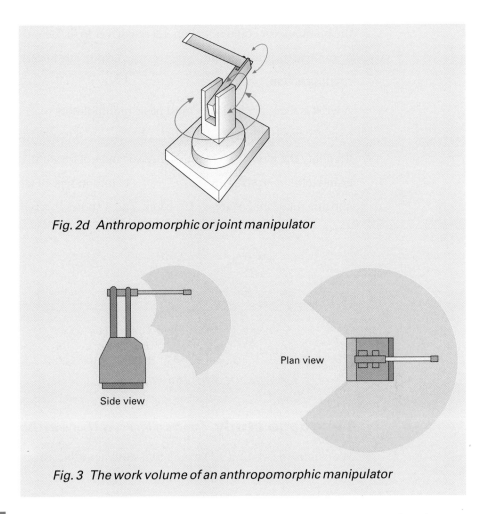

Fig. 2d Anthropomorphic or joint manipulator

Plan view

Side view

Fig. 3 The work volume of an anthropomorphic manipulator

Task 7

Now exchange information with the others in your group to complete the table.

Task 8

Complete the blanks in this text.

Mechanical wrist

It is worth pointing [1]_____ that a human arm has far more freedom [2]_____ the minimum three degrees of freedom, giving very great flexibility in terms [3]_____ positioning, path taken, and angle of approach. Even without a wrist, the redundant degrees of freedom of the [4]_____ body would allow you to carry out most normal operations. Any of the basic manipulators shown [5]_____ Figs. 2 a–d, on the other [6]_____, would be virtually useless as they stand. Although they could get to any position, they [7]_____ only approach objects from a single angle.

To take an [8]_____, removing a screw would be impossible [9]_____ the manipulator could not align a screwdriver to fit the screw properly. Even if it was able to, it still would [10]_____ be possible to carry out the necessary rotating action.

A wrist is therefore added to most basic manipulators to [11]_____ the required mechanical flexibility to [12]_____ real jobs. In general, for total flexibility the wrist itself requires three degrees of freedom, thereby bringing the grand total up to six. The [13]_____ common type of wrist has two bending and one rotational degrees of freedom. Fig. 4 shows this type of mechanical wrist.

Fig. 4 A typical mechanical wrist

Language study *Concession:* ***even if*** *and* ***although***

We can use *if* (see Unit 11) to link two statements like this:

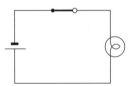

1   The switch is on.
2   The lamp lights.

If *the switch is on, the lamp lights.*

When statement 1 is true, statement 2 is also true.

When statement 1 surprisingly has no effect on statement 2, we can use *even if* or *although*. For example:

1   The switch is on.
2   The lamp does not light.

Even if *the switch is on, the lamp does not light.*
Although *the switch is on, the lamp does not light.*

A car is fitted with a seat belt warning light. The light operates under these conditions:

Seat occupied	Ignition	Belt	Light
Yes	On	Closed	Off
Yes	On	Open	On
Yes	Off	Closed	Off
No	Off	Closed	Off

Study these examples of normal and faulty operation:

Normal
If the seat is occupied, the ignition on and the belt closed, the light is off.

Faulty
Even if the belt is closed, the light stays on.
Although the belt is closed, the light stays on.

Give other examples of normal and faulty operation of this circuit.

Technical reading *Stepper motors*

Task 10

Read the text which follows to find the answers to these questions, then complete the table.

1 Why would you use a stepper motor to position the head of a disk drive unit?
2 Name two components that are present in other electric motor types but absent from stepper motors.
3 For accuracy in positioning, would you select a stepper motor with a large or a small step angle?

Type	Advantages	Applications
Variable reluctance	No detent torque	
_____	High dynamic torque at low speed	_____
Hybrid type	Good speed/torque characteristics	—
_____	Can be made very small, very efficient	_____

> Stepper motors are useful wherever accurate control of movement is required. They are used extensively in robotics and in printers, plotters and computer disk drives, all of which require precise positioning or speed. In a plotter, for example, by using two motors
> 5 running at 90 degrees to each other, they can be used to drive a pen an exact distance in all directions. In robotics, they are used to position manipulators exactly where required. ▶

A stepper motor does not run in the same way as a normal DC
motor, i.e. continuously rotating. Instead, it runs in a series of
10 measured steps. These steps are triggered by pulses from a
computer, each pulse making the motor turn either in a forward or
a reverse direction by an exact interval, typically 1.8, 2.5, 3.75, 7.5,
15, or 30 degrees. Accuracy is within 3% to 5% of the last step.

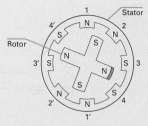

Fig. 5a   *Fig. 5b*

The rotor in a stepper motor is constructed from several permanent
15 magnets with north and south poles. The stator is wound into a
series of electromagnets, usually four, which can be switched on
and off. Figs. 5a and b illustrate the operation of a permanent
magnet-type stepper motor. When current is applied to the stator
coils, it creates the pole arrangement shown in Fig. 5a. Poles 1 and
20 2 are north. Hence, the rotor south pole is attracted to both of them
and settles in the mid position as shown. When the stator currents
are changed to produce the pole arrangement shown in Fig. 5b,
pole 1 has south polarity. This repels the rotor which moves to the
new position as shown. Each polarity change on the stator causes
25 the rotor to move (in this case) 45 degrees.

Stepper motors can be divided into two groups. The first one works
without a permanent magnet. The second one has a permanent
magnet, usually located on the rotor.

Variable reluctance motors form the first group. As there is no
30 permanent magnet, the variable reluctance motor has practically
no detent torque. The rotor spins freely and gives good
acceleration and high speed if lightly loaded. Applications include
micropositioning tables.

The second group comprise the permanent magnet motor, the
35 hybrid motor, and the disc magnet motor. The permanent magnet
type offers high dynamic torque at low speed and large step
angles. This is a low cost motor used extensively in low inertia
applications such as computer peripherals and printers.

The hybrid type combines features of both types mentioned above.
40 It has good speed/torque characteristics and micro-stepping
capability. Steps of 1.8 degrees are possible.

Disc magnet motors can be made very small and are very efficient.
One of their first applications was in quartz-controlled watches.

29 Careers in engineering

Tuning-in

Task 1

List some of the jobs in engineering. Combine your list with others in your group.

Task 2

Work in groups of three, **A**, **B**, and **C**. Scan your section of this text, **A**, **B**, or **C**. How many of the jobs in the combined list you made in Task 1 are mentioned in your section?

Jobs in engineering

A

Professional engineers may work as:

Design engineers: They work as part of a team to create new products and extend the life of old products by updating them and finding new applications for them. Their aim is to build quality and
5 reliability into the design and to introduce new components and materials to make the product cheaper, lighter, or stronger.

Installation engineers: They work on the customer's premises to install equipment produced by their company.

Production engineers: They ensure that the production process is
10 efficient, that materials are handled safely and correctly, and that faults which occur in production are corrected. The design and development departments consult with them to ensure that any innovations proposed are practicable and cost-effective. ▶

[handwritten annotations:]
relyon urself / self reliable
make it modern
goal/objective purpose
inefficient
able { to carry but / to get done } (formal)

165

[handwritten top margin: to specify = make pepople know about special thing.]

B

15 Just below the professional engineers are the *technician engineers*. They require a detailed knowledge of a particular technology – electrical, mechanical, electronic, etc. They may lead teams of engineering technicians. Technician engineers and engineering technicians may work as:

20 *Test/Laboratory technicians*: They test samples of the materials and of the product to ensure quality is maintained. *[handwritten: → production]*

Installation and service technicians: They ensure that equipment sold by the company is installed correctly and carry out *[handwritten: installation]* preventative maintenance and essential repairs. *[handwritten: important]* *[handwritten: to avoid]*

Production planning and control technicians: They produce the 25 manufacturing instructions and organize the work of production so that it can be done as quickly, cheaply, and efficiently as possible. *[handwritten: Production]*

Inspection technicians: They check and ensure that incoming and outgoing components and products meet specifications. *[handwritten: production]*

Debug technicians: They fault find, repair, and test equipment and 30 products down to component level. *[handwritten: Production]* *[handwritten left margin: find problems/mistake]*

Draughtsmen/women and designers: They produce the drawings and design documents from which the product is manufactured. *[handwritten: Design]*

C

The next grade are *craftsmen/women*. Their work is highly skilled and practical. Craftsmen and women may work as: *[handwritten: 3]*

25 *Toolmakers*: They make dies and moulding tools which are used to punch and form metal components and produce plastic components such as car bumpers. *[handwritten: → product the car-things]* *[handwritten: colors]*

Fitters: They assemble components into larger products.

Maintenance fitters: They repair machinery. *[handwritten: productions]*

40 *Welders*: They do specialized joining, fabricating, and repair work. *[handwritten: pro]*

Electricians: They wire and install electrical equipment. *[handwritten: installetion]*

Operators require fewer skills. Many operator jobs consist mainly of minding a machine, especially now that more and more processes are automated. However, some operators may have to 45 check components produced by their machines to ensure they are accurate. They may require training in the use of instruments such as micrometers, verniers, or simple 'go/no go' gauges. *[handwritten: → device used to measure stg]*

Source: Adapted from S. Moss & A.S. Watts, *Careers in Engineering*, 3rd edition

---

Task 3

Combine answers with the others in your group. How many of the jobs listed in Task 1 are mentioned in the whole text?

Task 4

Who would be employed to:
1 test completed motors from a production line? *[handwritten: test test laboratory]*
2 find out why a new electronics assembly does not work? *[handwritten: debug technician]*
3 produce a mould for a car body part? *[handwritten: toolmarkers]*
4 see that the correct test equipment is available on a production line? *[handwritten: pr]*
5 find a cheaper way of manufacturing a crankshaft? *[handwritten: production planing]*

6 repair heating systems installed by their company? *installatione service* *technician*

7 see that a new product is safe to use? *test technician*

8 commission a turbine in a power station? *installation engineering*

Reading *Inferring from samples*

In Task 5 below and in the Listening (Task 7), you are asked to infer from a small sample of text information which is not clearly stated. Use the clues in the samples and the knowledge you have gained from the text *Jobs in engineering*.

Task 5

As a group, try to identify the jobs of these workers from their statements.

1 We perform standard chemical and physical tests on samples, usually as a result of a complaint from inspectors on the production line. We are an important part of production. We have the authority to stop the line if we find something seriously wrong. It's interesting work, and we're able to
5 move around from test to test and chat. Sometimes, admittedly, the work gets a bit repetitive. *test laboratory technicians guys*

2 All machinists can be difficult. The older blokes especially don't like me *inspection* telling them their work isn't good enough and instructing them to do it again. One or two of them seem to think the inspector is always out to get
10 them. I'm constantly having to calm things down.

3 We measure up the components to see that they are the right size and *fitters* shape, and we make any minor adjustments ourselves with hand tools or power tools. All along, parts will need adjusting slightly and you have to check things at each stage with measuring instruments and gauges. You
15 have to get a feel for it – clearances have to be just right. Otherwise things won't fit together. *an object → the amount of space around that is necessary for it to avoid touching another object*

4 I find my job a very satisfying one. It's never easy to say exactly why one likes a job. I think the basic thing I get out of my profession at the moment is the creativity that is involved in design work. You start from square one
20 with a plain sheet of paper. You draw a component. You design something and perhaps a few months later you can see the end product. And you get told whether or not your design works! I think it's that aspect that I find most satisfying. *design engineering.*

5 I enjoy my job. I really like doing the same thing every day – exactly the
25 same job. You know what to look for and how things should be. You know how the machine – or the machines – run, when a machine is working properly and when there is something wrong with it. I really like the routine. I don't have dreams of becoming a supervisor or anything like that. I'm just content running my machines. *machine operator production planning*

6
30 My company makes desalination equipment. It takes the salt out of sea water so it can be used for drinking and irrigation. A lot of our customers are in the Middle East. I have to go there whenever new equipment is being set up to make sure it's properly installed and everything is running OK. *installation technician production planning*

Source (quotations 1–5): T. May, *People at Work: Working at a light engineering plant*

Speaking practice *Role play*

Task 6

Work in pairs, **A** and **B**. Each of you has profiles of three workers in a light engineering plant which supplies car electrical components such as starter motors, fuel pumps, and alternators.

Play the part of one of these workers and be prepared to answer questions from your partner about your work. Your partner must try to identify your job from your replies.

In turn, find out about your partner.

Do not give your partner your job title until he or she has found out as much information as possible and has made a guess at your occupation. Try to find out:

1 Age
2 Education
3 Qualifications
4 Nature of work
5 Who he/she is responsible to
6 What he/she feels about his/her work

Before you start, work out with your partner useful questions to obtain this information.

Student A: Your profile is on pages 179/80.
Student B: Your profile is on page 183.

Listening *Inferring from samples*

Task 7

Listen to these workers talking about their jobs. Try to match each extract to one of these jobs.

a Methods engineer
b Systems analyst
c Toolmaker
d Machine tool development fitter
e Foreman/woman
f Applications engineer

30 Applying for a job

Tuning-in

Task 1

What sort of engineering job do you do at present or would you like to do in the future? What are the attractions of the job? Compare answers with others in your group.

Reading *Understanding job advertisements*

Task 2

Answer the questions below about this job advertisement.

AAA ➤ Castleton Airport

As a highly successful part of AAA plc, we handled approximately 5 million passengers last year. Further expansion of the airport facilities has created a career opportunity for the following:

Engineering Technicians
c.£13,000

In this multi-skilled role you will carry out corrective and preventative maintenance on a variety of electrical, electronic, and mechanical plant. You will use computer-based monitoring systems for effective control, fault diagnosis, and operation of plant and equipment.

Applicants should have a recognized HNC or National Certificate in Electrical/Electronic Engineering and have served a recognized apprenticeship. Experience in the operation and maintenance of electro-mechanical plant utilizing electronic system control including experience of HVAC plant and systems, electronic PLC systems, boiler control systems, positional and electronic speed control systems including hydraulics, pumps, and heat exchangers would be desirable.

This demanding position requires effective communication skills together with a flexible attitude.

A clean current driving licence is essential.

In return you can expect an attractive salary and benefits package.

Please forward a comprehensive CV to Denise Dickens, Personnel Department, Administrative Block A, Castleton Airport, Castleton CS21 3SL. Closing date for receipt of completed applications is 31 December.

---

1 Which company is advertising?
2 Where are the jobs based?
3 At what professional level are the jobs available?
4 Applicants from which branch of engineering are eligible?
5 What qualifications are required?
6 In addition to qualifications, what must the applicants have completed?
7 List some of the areas in which experience is sought.
8 Might you be considered for the job without this experience?
9 In addition to qualifications and experience, what characteristics should applicants have?
10 Which non-professional qualification is essential?

11 What might a benefits package include?

12 What are PLC systems?

13 What does HVAC mean?

14 What is a CV?

Task 3

Fiona Weaver decides to apply for one of the posts. Study her CV below. Answer these questions.

1 What is her highest educational qualification?

2 Why do you think the education and experience sections of her CV start with the most recent events?

3 Why does she give two references?

4 Why has she chosen these people to be her referees?

5 Why does she include interests and activities?

```
CURRICULUM VITAE

Personal details
Name:            Fiona Weaver
Date of birth:   7 April 1974
Address:         6 Haymarket, Newcastle, NC1 4YU
Marital status:  Single

Education and qualifications
1991-1995        Faraday College of Further Education, Newcastle
                 - National Certificate in Electrical and Electronic Engineering
                   (day release from S & T (UK) Ltd)
1985-1990        George Stephenson Secondary School, Newcastle

I hold a clean driving licence. I have been driving for three years.

Work experience
1995 to present  Inspection Technician
                 Sturner & Thomson (UK) Ltd
                 - Responsible for checking incoming components and completed
                   products using a wide range of test equipment including
                   computer-based record systems.

1991-1995        Apprentice electrical technician
                 Sturner & Thomson (UK) Ltd

1990-1991        Office junior
                 Brent & Wicker, Solicitors
                 - Basic secretarial duties-filing, word-processing, telephone
                   receptionist, in a busy lawyer's office

Interests and activities
                 Travel, modern dance, swimming

References        College:                  Work:
                 Mr Andrew Wood            Mrs Joy Milne
                 Head of Department        Personnel Officer
                 Electrical Engineering    S & T (UK) Ltd
                 Faraday College           North Street
                 Cornwallis Road           NEWCASTLE NC14 7TL
                 NEWCASTLE NC2 3PL
```

Study this letter of application which accompanied the CV. What information does it add to the CV?

---

6 Haymarket
Newcastle
NC1 4YU

p.o 87873 dubai

15 December 19—

Ms Denise Dickens
Personnel Department
Administrative Block A
Castleton Airport
Castleton CS21 3SL

KC/O darestani   p.o 5085 dubai uae

Dear·Ms Dickens,

Re: Engineering Technicians

I would like to apply for the post of Engineering Technician as advertised in today's issue of the Tribune. I enclose my CV with the names of two referees.

You will note from my CV that I have a National Certificate in Electrical and Electronic Engineering and considerable experience. My work at S & T (UK) means that I am familiar with HVAC plant and systems including electronic system control. As an inspection technician, I have experience of a wide range of systems for product testing and component evaluation.

I enjoy my work at S & T but would like now to broaden my experience, especially in the area of maintenance. I feel that I can bring considerable skill to the post together with the ability to work well in a team. I am also interested in further improving my qualifications by studying for an HNC, part-time.

I look forward to hearing from you.
Yours sincerely

Fiona Weaver *2000-2002 work as accountant*   *expience:*
2001-2002
Fiona Weaver *2002-2004 in a Conveyor.* *2002-2004 Capable*
2004-2005   *of running*
in Construction
Company   *work as an   in Emar*
Company

Speaking practice *Role play*

Task 5

Imagine you are Ms Dickens of Castleton Airport. List Fiona's strong points and weak points. Plan questions to ask her at her interview.

Task 6

Now divide into pairs so that you are working with another student. Act out the interview with one being the applicant and the other the personnel officer. You can change Ms Dickens to Mr Dickens and Fiona Weaver to Michael Weaver if you wish.

Task 7

Study the advertisements on the following pages. Select suitable jobs for which these applicants could apply.

1   Technician engineer, 27, HNC in Electrical Engineering, with two years' sales experience.
2   Professional engineer, 35, with five years' experience in the automotive industry.
3   Design engineer, 42, BSc in Mechanical Engineering, with experience in managing projects both in-house and subcontracted.
4   Technician, 24, National Certificate in Mechanical Engineering, two years' shop floor experience.
5   Electrical engineer, 50, HNC, long experience in maintenance of high voltage plant.
6   Mechanical engineer, 46, HND, experience in maintenance.
7   Yourself.

SALES ENGINEER

Sinclair is one of the UK's largest private engineering groups, with an international reputation. The sealing systems operation requires a Technical Sales Engineer to sell the world-renowned Chesterfield range of products throughout the Midlands.

You should have previous sales and mechanical engineering experience with a bias to maintenance products and mechanical engineering.

The successful candidate will ideally be between 30 and 45 years of age living in the Midlands with a mechanical engineering background.

The company offer a good basic salary, commission and company car. Apply in writing, with full cv to:
J. FORD
SINCLAIR SEALING SYSTEMS LTD.
16 CANYON ROAD, NETHERTON INDUSTRIAL ESTATE, BIRMINGHAM B2 0ER   Closing date 17 December 19—

SINCLAIR

PROJECT/DESIGN ENGINEER

We are a long established medium/heavy engineering company (Liverpool area) specializing in mechanical handling equipment and require to appoint a project/design engineer for our busy drawing office.

The applicant should be aged between 28 and 40 and must have a sound and practical engineering background. Ideally he/she should be a time served draughtsperson, capable of running projects from initial concept, through design and detail including to final installation. He/She should have experience in fork truck attachments, lifting beams, and conveyor systems; must be able to work on his/her own initiative and liaise with customers. This is an extremely responsible position with good prospects for further advancement.

Please reply in writing with full cv in the first instance to Box 1383, The Herald, Liverpool L1 1QP.

a   6   b   3

c

d

PREMIER PV VANDERBILT

A Division of N & S plc

Part of the N & S Group, one of the world's major suppliers of automotive components, PREMIER VANDERBILT LTD is a market leader in the manufacture of plain bearings for automotive and general engineering applications.

QUALITY ENGINEER – c. £16k

Our manufacturing facility at Wycliffe Valley, Bathgate, commenced production in early 1992 and the workforce has expanded rapidly. We now require a Quality Engineer to join us.

Reporting to the Quality Assurance Manager, you will be responsible for ensuring quality related activities are implemented in line with company policies and objectives.

Educated to at least HNC level in mechanical engineering, experience in quality improvement in the automotive industry would be a distinct advantage. A working knowledge of SPC, FMEA, DOE, and problem solving techniques is essential.

Together with an attractive salary the benefits are those which can be expected from a progressive organization. There will be excellent opportunities for career development as the company continues to grow.

To apply, please send a cv stating current salary, to, Stuart P. Alexander, Human Resources Manager, Premier Vanderbilt Ltd, 10 Stonehouse Road, Wycliffe Valley Industrial Estate, Bathgate, Berks RG20 2EW.

Closing date for applications is Wednesday 5 January 19 — and interviews will be held during January 19 —.

e

Write your CV and a letter of application for one of the posts advertised in Task 7. You may invent suitable qualifications and experience if you are still a student.

Technical reading *Company structure*

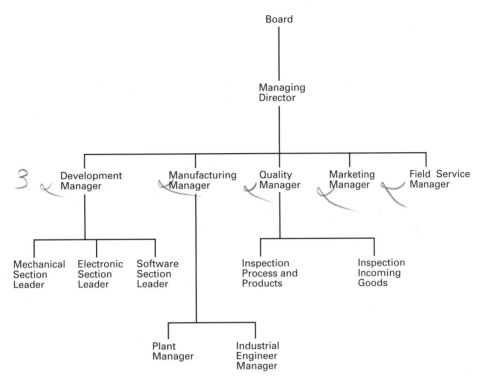

Fig. 1

Complete the blanks in this text using information from Fig. 1.

The head of an engineering company in the UK is the ^{1}_____ or the Chief Executive Officer (CEO). If it is an American subsidiary, the head may be known as the Vice President. Unless the person at the top is the Chairman of the company, or the owner, he or she will be responsible to a ^{2}_____, or, in the case of a US subsidiary, the President. In turn, the Chairman or President is responsible to the company shareholders.

The managers of the various departments which are vital to a company report directly to the Managing Director. These managers may be referred to as the Management Team. They are required to advise the Director on the consequences of any decision made by the Board in terms of costs, personnel, materials, time, plant, etc. They also have to brief the Director on any matters which should be taken to the Board for decision.

The 3 _____, with the support of the Mechanical, Electronic, and 4 _____ Sections, is responsible for the introduction of new products. The 5 _____ decides how the new products will be produced. The 6 _____ and Industrial Engineer Manager report to this member of the Management Team.

The 7 _____ ensures that the products are fault-free and that the components and materials used in their manufacture meet company standards. The 8 _____ handles market research, promotion, and sales. The Field Service Manager is responsible for the installation and maintenance of the company's products wherever required.

The structure shown in Fig. 1 is common to most engineering companies but there can be differences in reporting channels. For example, in some companies the Field Service Department may report through Marketing, through Quality, or even through a separate Product Assurance and Support Group.

Although the company structure shows managers for each separate department, departments are interdependent. For example, the Development Manager would not start the design of a new product without first discussing the project with other managers. The design would not be completed without regular meetings with other departments to ensure that it fitted the customers' requirements, and that cost targets would be met without adversely affecting quality, manufacturability, and serviceability. These meetings would ensure that trained manpower, tooling, documentation, etc., were in place at the correct time for each stage of the product's launch.

Task 10

Read the text again to find the answers to these questions.

1 What is the US equivalent of the Managing Director?
2 Who is the Chairman of a company responsible to?
3 Who comprise the Management Team?
4 In what way might companies differ in structure from the example given?
5 Which department would advise on whether a new product would meet customers' requirements?

Student A
Speaking practice

Unit 4

Task 7

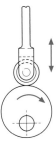

Unit 12

Task 10

Use this text and diagrams to help you. Your partner has the same diagrams but without the text. Make sure your instructions are simple and clear.

Adjusting the distance between the saddle and the handlebars

It is important that the distance between the saddle and the handlebars should suit the rider.

Place the elbow at the point of the saddle and stretch out your arm and hand. The distance between the handlebars and the fingertips
5 should be approximately 5 cm. If necessary, slide the saddle forwards or backwards after loosening nuts A.

When re-tightening, make sure the saddle remains in an almost horizontal position and see that it is properly centred.

After re-tightening, ensure that the saddle is secured firmly and
10 cannot be moved.

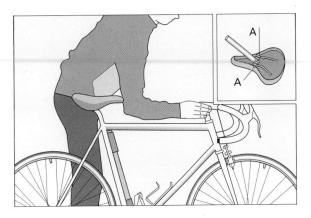

This diagram will help you to understand your partner's explanation.

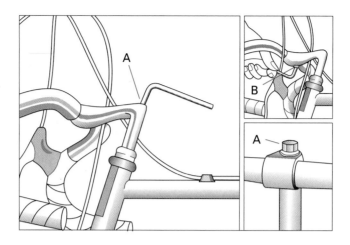

Unit 14

Task 6

Complete the missing design specifications.

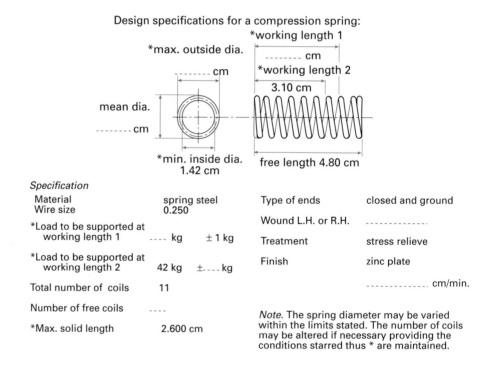

Design specifications for a compression spring:

*working length 1

*max. outside dia.

-------- cm

*working length 2

3.10 cm

mean dia.

-------- cm

*min. inside dia.
1.42 cm

free length 4.80 cm

Specification

Material	spring steel		Type of ends	closed and ground
Wire size	0.250			
			Wound L.H. or R.H.	--------------
*Load to be supported at working length 1	---- kg	± 1 kg	Treatment	stress relieve
			Finish	zinc plate
*Load to be supported at working length 2	42 kg	±---- kg		
				------------- cm/min.
Total number of coils	11			
Number of free coils	----			
*Max. solid length	2.600 cm			

Note. The spring diameter may be varied within the limits stated. The number of coils may be altered if necessary providing the conditions starred thus * are maintained.

Unit 18

Indicates

Indicates
exhaust

Indicates
air supply

Symbol
for

Symbol
for SAC

Indicates

Indicates
spring return

Indicates

Unit 22

Pitting describes the form of corrosion where localized grains of metal are consumed, leaving small, irregular, but possibly deep, holes.

Although the amount of material removed may be small, the metal may be perforated.

Galvanic corrosion results where two dissimilar metals are connected in the presence of moisture producing an electrolytic cell. The more active metal becomes the anode and corrodes away, while the less active will be protected.

Unit 29

1   Choose from one of these three profiles.

a   Age   22

Job title   Machine tool development fitter.

Education   College of Technology, full Technician's Certificate by day release over 4 years.

Duties   Works on automatic machines in the machine tool development department, one of 17 millers, turners, and grinders. Responsible for maintenance of machines, making jigs, and fixtures for specialist jobs and for building and commissioning new machines.

Responsible to   Foreman

Likes/dislikes   Likes the job because of the variety of work.

b   Age   42

Job title   General foreman/woman

Education   Technical college, City & Guilds Certificate by day release.

Duties   Is in charge of 26 people – machine tool operators, tool setters, etc. Based on the shop floor. Controls everyday production jobs.

Responsible to   Superintendent

Likes/dislikes   Doesn't like having to sack people.

c Age 22

Job title Applications engineer

Education Technical college, City & Guilds Certificate by day release over 4 years

Duties Works in applications department – around 30 people. Responsible for liaison between the company and the customer. Tries to ensure that the customer's requirements can be met by the company's products. Carries out tests on the products and sends results to the customer on how the product performs.

Responsible to Department manager

Likes/dislikes Gets a lot of job satisfaction because he/she gets to see an end result. Finds the systems in the factory a bit cumbersome. They can hold up the work of the section.

2 Your partner is one of these workers:

Methods engineer
Systems analyst
Tool maker

Student B
Speaking practice

Unit 4

Task 7

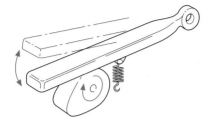

Unit 12

Task 10 Use this text and diagrams to help you. Your partner has the same diagrams but has no text. Make sure your instructions are simple and clear.

> **Adjusting the handlebar height and tilt**
>
> A comfortable position is the best test. Different heights and angles of the handlebars should be tried until you find the position which most suits you.
>
> To adjust the height, unscrew the expander bolt A by three or four
> 5 turns. Give a sharp blow to the bolt head to loosen the handlebars. Re-tighten once the proper height is obtained.
>
> Make sure the handlebars stem is not pulled too far out of the frame tube. The stem must remain at least 65 mm engaged in the front fork. The grooved part of the expansion slits should not show.
>
> 10 To tilt the handlebars, loosen bolt B.
>
> After all adjustments have been made, make sure both bolts are firmly secured with the correct tools. The handlebars should not twist when the front wheel is held firmly between the knees.

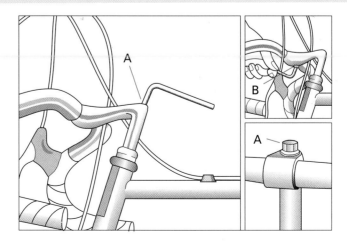

This diagram will help you to understand your partner's explanation.

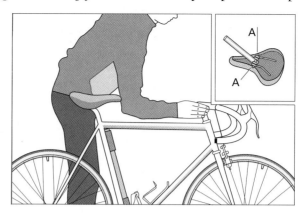

Unit 14

Task 6

Complete the missing design specifications.

Design specifications for a compression spring:

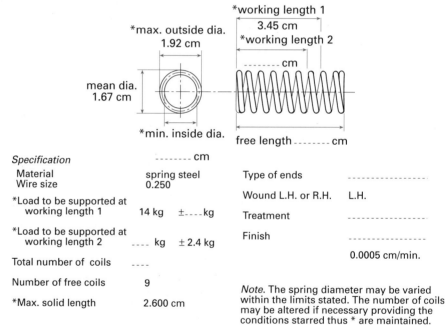

Specification	
Material	spring steel
Wire size	0.250
*Load to be supported at working length 1	14 kg ±----kg
*Load to be supported at working length 2	---- kg ± 2.4 kg
Total number of coils	----
Number of free coils	9
*Max. solid length	2.600 cm

Type of ends	-----------------
Wound L.H. or R.H.	L.H.
Treatment	-----------------
Finish	-----------------
	0.0005 cm/min.

Note. The spring diameter may be varied within the limits stated. The number of coils may be altered if necessary providing the conditions starred thus * are maintained.

Unit 18

Task 13

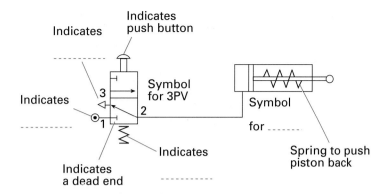

Indicates push button

Indicates

Symbol for 3PV

Indicates

3

2

1

Symbol for ⸱⸱⸱⸱⸱⸱⸱

Spring to push piston back

Indicates

Indicates a dead end

Unit 22

Task 6

Demetallification is the effective removal of one metal from an alloy, such as zinc from a copper–zinc alloy.

Although the metal remaining after attack retains similar dimensions to the original, it lacks mechanical strength and is porous.

Microbiological corrosion is more often found in hot countries, but it also occurs in tanks, such as fuel tanks. Fungus enters through the ventilation system or with the fuel and grows inside the tank. This leads to leakage and can result in structural failure.

Unit 29

Task 6

1 Choose from one of these three profiles.

a
Age	28
Job title	Methods engineer
Education	FE College, Higher National Diploma, (a sandwich course – 6 months work, 6 months study). University, BSc (Eng).
Duties	Part of a team which plans new components and how they are to be manufactured. Also responsible for specifying or recommending new equipment and new machines. If there is a problem with production or materials used for a project, the team has to sort it out.
Responsible to	Production engineering manager
Likes/dislikes	Enjoys working as part of a team and solving problems.

b	Age 24
Job title	Systems analyst
Education	Polytechnic, BA in Business Studies
Duties	Assistant analyst in management services department. Part of a team composed of analysts and programmers. When a department has a problem, he/she has to analyse it and come up with a solution. If it is a solution which can be solved by a computer, the team design, write, and test a computer program for the problem. If it goes well, the program is put into use. This may involve training a 'user' in the new system.
Responsible to	Section leader
Likes/dislikes	Enjoys working with so many departments. Doesn't like it when a user changes his/her mind about something after hours have been spent designing a system.
c	Age 23
Job title	Toolmaker
Education	College of Technology, City & Guilds sandwich course
Duties	One of 50 who work in the tool room – fitters, turners, millers, grinder, jig borers. Spends time on each kind of machine – surface grinders, lathe, mill.
Responsible to	Foreman/woman
Likes/dislikes	Likes working with his/her hands. Enjoys getting experience with different kinds of machines.

2   Your partner is one of these workers:

Machine tool development fitter
Foreman/woman
Applications engineer

Glossary of engineering terms and abbreviations

The definitions in this glossary refer to words only as they are used in this book. The meanings of certain words will vary according to context. As the texts in this book are authentic and come from a variety of sources, some inconsistency in hyphenation and spelling is inevitable.

The unit and task numbers indicate where the word first appears.

Abbreviations used in the text

R = Reading section
SP = Speaking practice
T = Task
TS = Tapescript
U = Unit
W = Writing section

n = noun
adj = adjective
v = verb

A-frame /'eɪ freɪm/ *n* [U10, T5] a structural frame in the shape of the letter A

ac /eɪ 'si:/ *n* [U23, T6] alternating current

aerodynamic /ˌeərəʊdaɪ'næmɪk/ *adj* [U12, T3] designed to reduce wind resistance

air classifier /'eə ˌklæsɪfaɪə(r)/ *n* [U27, T3] a machine which uses air to segregate materials by size and weight

alarm /ə'lɑːm/ *n* [U11, T3] a means of attracting attention utilizing either sound or vision

alloy /'ælɔɪ/ *n* [U12, T3] a metal formed by mixing together other metals and elements

alternator /'ɔːltəneɪtə(r)/ *n* [U17, T3] a type of generator producing alternating current

amplifier /'æmplɪfaɪə(r)/ *n* [U16, T8] an electronic device which converts small signal changes to large

anthropomorphic /ˌænθrəpə'mɔːfɪk/ *n* [U28, T3] of human-like form

armature /'ɑːmətʃə(r)/ *n* [U6, T2] the moving part of an electric motor which comprises a piece of iron with loops of wire running round it; the current through the wire is reversed to provide the changes in magnetic fields required to make the motor run

bearing /'beərɪŋ/ *n* [U2, T4] a device to reduce friction and wear between a rotating shaft and a stationary part; may contain balls or rollers

bimetallic corrosion /ˌbaɪmətælɪk kə'rəʊʒn/ *n* [U22, T6] *see* galvanic corrosion

block diagram /'blɒk ˌdaɪəgræm/ *n* [U11, T3] schematic drawing showing different functions in a system or stages in a process

body scanner /'bɒdi ˌskænə(r)/ *n* [U1, T4] a medical electronic device for building up an image of the internal organs of a patient

brittle /'brɪtl/ *adj* [U3, T2] describes a material which tends to break easily, e.g. glass

brushes /'brʌʃɪz/ *n* [U6, T2] spring-loaded carbon blocks which carry the electric current to the commutator of an electric motor

buoyancy /'bɔɪənsɪ/ *n* [U5, T3] the upthrust exerted by a fluid

buzzer /'bʌzə(r)/ *n* [U7, T5 TS] a device which uses an electric signal to produce a buzzing sound

C

CAD /kæd/ *n* [U20, T1] Computer-Aided Design

CAM /kæm/ *n* [U20, T2] Computer-Aided Manufacture

cam /kæm/ *n* [U4, T7] a specially profiled part which is fitted to a rotating shaft to produce linear motion

capillary tube /kə'pɪlərɪ ˌtjuːb/ *n* [U15, T2] a tube with a very small diameter bore

CAPP /kæp/ *n* [U20, T2] Computer-Aided Process Planning

carbon fibre /'kɑːbn ˌfaɪbə(r)/ *n* [U25, T5] high-strength fibre made from carbon atoms

carburettor /ˌkɑːbə'retə(r)/ *n* [U17, T3] a device where air and petrol are mixed in an internal combustion engine

Cartesian co-ordinates /kɑːˌtiːʒn kəʊ'ɔːdɪnəts/ *n* [U28, T5] information about the position of a body in space using distances measured from three intersecting planes

chain wheel /'tʃeɪn wiːl/ *n* [U12, T1] a toothed pulley or sprocket used for transmitting torque by a chain

charger /'tʃɑːdʒə(r)/ *n* [U15, T4] a device which contains a unit for converting mains power to direct current at a suitable voltage for charging batteries

chisel /'tʃɪzl/ *n* [U18, T3] a steel tool with one end formed into a cutting edge

CIM /sɪm/ *n* [U20, T1] Computer-Integrated Manufacturing: describes a series of processes or activities co-ordinated by using a computer

circuit breaker /'sɜːkɪt ˌbreɪkə(r)/ *n* [U21, T6] an electrical switch fitted with an overload protection cut out

closed loop /ˌkləʊzd'luːp/ *n* [U11, T3] a system where part of the output of a system is fed back into the input to modify the output

commutator /'kɒmjuːˌteɪtə(r)/ *n* [U6, T2] the part of the armature of an electric motor which is in contact with the brushes; it reverses the flow of current through the armature

compact disc /ˌkɒmpækt 'dɪsk/ *n* [U13, T2] plastic disc used to store high quality sound recordings or computer data on its surface

component evaluation /kəmˌpəʊnənt ɪvæljʊ'eɪʃn/ *n* [U30, T4] the testing of a component to ensure it conforms to specifications

composite /'kɒmpəzɪt/ *n* [U25, T4] a fibre-reinforced plastic material

compressed air /kəmˌprest'eə(r)/ *n* [U18, T1] air at higher than atmospheric pressure; used to power pneumatic devices such as drills

compression /kəm'preʃn/ *n* [U4, T4] the effect of forces which act to squash a structure

computer model /kəm'pjuːtə ˌmɒdl/ *n* [U24, T7] a representation of a design created in 3D on a computer using a CAD programme

computer-based /kəm'pjuːtə ˌbeɪst/ *adj* [U30, T3] describes a system which relies on the use of a computer

condenser /kən'densə(r)/ *n* [U15, T2] a unit where vapour is converted back into a liquid

conductor /kən'dʌktə(r)/ *n* [U3, T3] a material which will transmit electricity or heat

constraint /kən'streɪnt/ *n* [U28, T6] limit imposed by the nature of a mechanism

cooling duct /'kuːlɪŋ dʌkt/ *n* [U23, T9] a passageway to allow air to pass to a hot surface, for example, in a motor

corrosion-resistant /kə'rəʊʒn rɪˌzɪstənt/ *adj* [U3, T3] describes a material which can be used in environments where long-term strength or appearance is important, e.g. stainless steel

corrosive /kə'rəʊsɪv/ *adj* [U9, T1] describes a substance which corrodes (eats or wears away), usually by chemical action

crankshaft /'krænkʃɑːft/ *n* [U4, T2] the main shaft of an engine which carries the cranks for the pistons

crevice corrosion /'krevɪs kəˌrəʊʒn/ *n* [U22, T6] corrosion in cracks or crevices in pipes carrying liquids

cylinder head /'sɪlɪndə ˌhed/ *n* [U3, W] a plate which seals the ends of cylinders on internal combustion engines; it contains the valves

D

damper /'dæmpə(r)/ *n* [U23, T2] a device fitted between the chassis and axle of a vehicle to remove spring effects and smooth travel

database /'deɪtəbeɪs/ *n* [U20, T2] a bank of information stored in a computer for easy access

dc /di: 'si:/ *n* [U6, T5] direct current

debug /ˌdi:'bʌg/ *vt* [U29, T2] detect, locate and correct faults

degrees of freedom /dɪˌgri:z əv 'fri:dəm/ *n* [U28, T4] the movements achievable by a robot in three-dimensional space

desalination /ˌdi:sælɪ'neɪʃn/ *n* [U29, T5] production of fresh water from sea water

die /daɪ/ *n* [U13, T7] a specially shaped block of metal used as a mould for other materials

die-cast /'daɪkɑ:st/ *adj* [U12, T6] produced from moulds

disc brakes /'dɪsk breɪks/ *n* [U19, T2] brakes in which a caliper clamps brake pads onto a disc connected to the wheel of the vehicle

diverter valve /daɪ'vɜ:tə ˌvælv/ *n* [U8, T6] a valve used in central heating to redirect the flow of hot water from radiators to water heating and vice versa

documentation /ˌdɒkjʊmen'teɪʃn/ *n* [U30, T9] the complete description of a product in words and drawings at every stage in its manufacture

ductile /'dʌktaɪl/ *adj* [U3, T3] describes a material which can be stretched and yet retain its strength, e.g. copper

ductility /dʌk'tɪlɪtɪ/ *n* [U26, T9] quality of being ductile

E

EDM /ˌi: di: 'em/ *n* [U20, T2] Engineering Data Management

elastic limit /ɪ'læstɪk ˌlɪmɪt/ *n* [U26, T6] the point at which a material will no longer return to its original shape after tensile forces are released

elasticity /ɪlæs'tɪsɪtɪ/ *n* [U5, T3] the property of a material to stretch and then return to its original state

encapsulation /ɪnˌkæpsjʊ'leɪʃn/ *n* [U3, T3] the process of completely embedding a component in a resin as protection from the environment

F

engine /'endʒɪn/ *n* [U3, W] a device which coverts fuel into work

equilibrium /ˌekwɪ'lɪbrɪəm/ *n* [U5, T3] balance (a structure is in equilibrium when all the forces on it are stable and there is no movement)

escalator /'eskəleɪtə(r)/ *n* [U4, T2] moving stairs

evaporator /ɪ'væpəreɪtə(r)/ *n* [U15, T2] a unit in which a liquid is converted into a vapour

exfoliate corrosion /eks'fəʊlɪət kəˌrəʊʒn/ *n* [U22, T6] when flakes of metal are displaced due to corrosion

extrusion /ɪk'stru:ʒn/ *n* [U13, T7] a manufacturing process whereby a material in its plastic state is forced through a die, e.g. to make plastic pipes

feedback /'fi:dbæk/ *n* [U11, T3] a signal responding to the output of a system which is returned to the input to modify the output

field magnet /'fi:ld ˌmægnət/ *n* [U6, T2] a magnet for producing and maintaining the magnetic field in a generator or electric motor

friction /'frɪkʃn/ *n* [U5, T2] the resistance experienced when two bodies rub against each other

fuel cell /'fjʊəl sel/ *n* [U25, T4] a cell which converts the chemical energy of a fuel to electrical energy

fulcrum /'fʊlkrəm/ *n* [U5, T6] the pivot point of a system of levers, e.g. the screw in a pair of scissors

G

galvanic corrosion /gæl'vænɪk kəˌrəʊʒn/ *n* [U22, T6] the corrosion which results when two dissimilar metals are connected in the presence of moisture

gears /gɪəz/ *n* [U12, T1] an arrangement of toothed wheels which mesh together to change the speed or direction of movement

goggles /'gɒgəlz/ *n* [U9, T7] protective eye wear completely surrounding the eyes

granules /'grænjʊəlz/ *n* [U13, T7] material, e.g. plastic, in the form of small grains

grinder /'graɪndə(r)/ n 1 [U9, T3] a machine with a rotating disc of abrasive material used for sharpening tools and removing rough edges [U29 SP (A)] a grinding machine operator

guard /ɡɑːd/ n [U9, T3] a device to safeguard the operators of moving machinery

hammer mill /'hæmə mɪl/ n [U27, T3] a crushing machine using impacts from rotating arms

hazard /'hæzəd/ n [U9, T2] danger

heat exchanger /'hiːt ɪksˌtʃeɪndʒə(r)/ n [U8, T3] the part of a boiler where the water is heated

heat-resistant /'hiːt rɪˌzɪstənt/ adj [U3, T3] describes a material which will withstand exposure to high temperature

hinge /hɪndʒ/ n [U5, T6] a flexible mounting for doors and lids

hydraulic /haɪ'drɔːlɪk/ adj [U19, T2] describes a system using cylinders and pistons and driven by a fluid

ignition /ɪɡ'nɪʃn/ n [U28, T9] the circuit which allows high-tension current to pass to the sparking plugs in an internal combustion engine

insulator /'ɪnsjʊˌleɪtə(r)/ n [U3, T3] a substance which will not transmit electricity or heat

interface /'ɪntəfeɪs/ n [U28, T2] hardware and software to enable a computer to communicate with the device to be controlled

intergranular corrosion /ˌɪntəɡrænjʊlə kə'rəʊʒn/ n [U22, T6] corrosion at the boundaries of the crystal grains of a material

IT /aɪ 'tiː/ n [U20, T1] Information Technology

jig /dʒɪɡ/ n [U29 SP (A)] a work-holding device made for a specific component, e.g. to hold it for drilling

JIT /ˌdʒeɪ aɪ 'tiː/ n [U20, T2] Just-In-Time manufacturing

laser /'leɪzə(r)/ n [U13, T2] Light Amplification by Stimulated Emission of Radiation

LCD /ˌel siː 'diː/ n [U16, T6] Liquid Crystal Display

load cell /'ləʊd sel/ n [U16, T5] a load-measuring element using an electrical strain gauge as the measuring device

malleable /'mælɪəbl/ adj [U3, T3] describes a material which can be stretched without breaking apart, e.g. copper

manipulator /mə'nɪpjʊˌleɪtə(r)/ n [U28, T2] the part of a robot which carries out the work

methods engineer /'meθədz endʒɪˌnɪə(r)/ n [U29, T7] someone concerned with establishing the best production method and equipment for making an article

micrometer /maɪ'krɒmɪtə(r)/ n [U29, T2] a U-shaped gauge used for precise measurement of thicknesses; the gap between the measuring faces is adjusted by rotating a screw thread encased in a graduated sleeve

microprocessor /ˌmaɪkrəʊ'prəʊsesə(r)/ n [U16, T5] integrated circuit chip at the centre of a computer for controlling the system and processing the data

mill /mɪl/ n [U29, SP (B)] a milling machine; uses multi-toothed cutters to shape metals and plastics

miller /'mɪlə(r)/ n [U29, SP (A)] a milling machine operator

MRP /ˌem ɑː 'piː/ n [U20, T2] materials requirement planning

pedal /'ped(ə)l/ n [U12, T1] foot-operated lever, e.g. the accelerator pedal of a car

pendulum /'pendjʊləm/ n [U4, T2] the swinging weight used for time control in some clocks

pilot light /'paɪlət laɪt/ n [U8, T2] a small flame used to ignite the main burners in a gas-fired heating boiler

pitch /pɪtʃ/ n [U28, T8] angular displacement along the lateral axis

pitting /'pɪtɪŋ/ n [U22, T6] corrosion due to localized chemical reaction

plant /plɑːnt/ n [U8, T7] the machines in a factory and all the buildings

PLC /ˌpiː el 'siː/ n [U20, T2] Programmable Logic Control/controller: the system/device by which a microprocessor controls a stage in a process automatically

pneumatic drill /njuːˌmætɪk 'drɪl/ n [U18, T3] a drilling machine using compressed air for power

pressure regulator /'preʃə ˌreɡjʊleɪtə(r)/ n [U21, T6] a device for adjusting or maintaining pressure levels

prototype /'prəʊtəˌtaɪp/ n [U10, T2 TS] the first working model

pulley /'pʊlɪ/ n [U10, T5] a grooved wheel over which a rope passes

R

reaction /ri:'æk∫n/ *n* [U5, T3] the force which opposes an applied force

reamer /ri:mə(r)/ *n* [U19, T6] a tool for enlarging a drilled hole to a precise diameter

recycling /ˌri:'saɪklɪŋ/ *n* [U27, T1] extracting from waste all materials that can be reprocessed to be used again

refrigerant /rɪ'frɪdʒərənt/ *n* [U15, T2] a substance which changes easily from a liquid to a gas and which can be used in refrigeration to remove heat energy and transfer it to the surroundings

regenerative braking /rɪ'dʒenərətɪv ˌbreɪkɪŋ/ *n* [U25, T5] a method of braking electric motors where the motor becomes a generator converting the energy of the slowing wheels into electricity

remote control /rɪˌməʊt kən'trəʊl/ *n* [U11, T3] a device for controlling something from a distance

respirator /'respəˌreɪtə(r)/ *n* [U9, T7] a mask worn over the nose and mouth to filter air

resultant /rɪ'zʌltənt/ *n* [U5, T2] the single outcome of a number of different vectors

revolve /rɪ'vɒlv/ *vi* [U5, T7 TS] turn, rotate

robotics /rəʊ'bɒtɪks/ *n* [U28] the study or production of machines which perform tasks in a manner similar to humans

roll /rəʊl/ *n* [U28, T8] angular rotation about a longitudinal axis

rotor /'rəʊtə(r)/ *n* [U17, T2] rotating part of a generator

S

scallop /'skɒləp/ *n* [U28, T6] fan-shaped curve

scratch-resistant /'skræt∫ rɪˌzɪstənt/ *adj* [U3, T3] describes a material which retains its appearance when exposed to abrasion

sensing device /'sensɪŋ dɪˌvaɪs/ *n* [U7, T5 TS] a device which monitors the operating environment and is sensitive to change

shock absorber /'∫ɒk əbˌzɔ:bə(r)/ *n* [U11, T2] a device for absorbing shocks and vibrations

signal generator /'sɪgnəl ˌdʒenəreɪtə(r)/ *n* [U21, T6] electronic device which produces various signals used in tests and measurements

solenoid /'səʊlənɔɪd/ *n* [U11, T2] a coil with an iron core which is pulled into the coil by a current passing through the coil

solenoid valve /'səʊlənɔɪd ˌvælv/ *n* [U11, T2] a valve operated by a solenoid

spanner /'spænə(r)/ *n* [U5, T7 TS] a tool, or level, for applying force to nuts and bolts

speed governor /'spi:dˌgʌvənə(r)/ *n* [U21, T6] a device fitted to an engine to limit its speed to a pre-set level

spring balance /ˌsprɪŋ 'bæləns/ *n* [U5, T3] a measuring device in which the force applied is calculated by the extension of a spring

sprocket /'sprɒkɪt/ *n* [U12, T10] a toothed wheel over which a chain passes

stator /'steɪtə(r)/ *n* [U17, T2] stationary part of a generator

strain gauge /'streɪn geɪdʒ/ *n* [U16, T5] a device for measuring strain in a structure

switchgear /'swɪt∫gɪə(r)/ *n* [U1, T5] switches and associated equipment for controlling large electrical currents

systems analyst /'sɪstəmz ˌænəlɪst/ *n* [U29, T7] someone responsible for examining a problem to see whether it is suitable for a computer application

T

tachogenerator /'tækəʊˌdʒenəreɪtə(r)/ *n* [U11, T4] a sensor for measuring the speed of rotation

TEFC /ˌti: i: ef 'si:/ *adj* [U23, T9] Totally-Enclosed Fan-Cooled (motor)

tension /'ten∫n/ *n* [U4, T4] the effect of a pulling force which tends to stretch a body

thermoplastic /'θɜ:məʊˌplæstɪk/ *n* [U3, T1] a plastic which softens when heated and hardens when cooled

thermosetting plastic /ˌθɜ:məʊsetɪŋ 'plæstɪk/ *n* [U3, T3] a plastic which retains its shape and rigidity at high temperatures

thermostat /'θɜ:məstæt/ *n* [U8, T3] a control device which operates at a pre-set temperature

throttle /'θrɒtl/ *n* [U18, T3] a valve for controlling the supply of a gas or liquid (e.g. fuel) to an engine

thrust /θrʌst/ *n* [U12, T6] force of propulsion

tooling /ˈtuːlɪŋ/ *n* [U13, T10] all manufacturing equipment required for the manufacture of a product

toxic /ˈtɒksɪk/ *adj* [U9, T1] poisonous

transformer /ˌtrænsˈfɔːmə(r)/ *n* [U6, T6] a device for stepping up or down the voltage of an alternating current

treadle /tredl/ *n* [U4, T6] a linkage used to convert oscillating into rotary movement and vice versa

turbine /ˈtɜːbaɪn/ *n* [U17, T9] a machine which produces power when steam, gas, or what is passed over the blades attached to the rotating drive output shaft

turbulence /ˈtɜːbjʊləns/ *n* [U12, T6] violent or uneven movement of air

turner /ˈtɜːnə(r)/ *n* [U29, SP (A)] a lathe operator

undercarriage /ˈʌndəˌkærɪdʒ/ *n* [U23, R2] the supporting framework of a vehicle comprising wheels, axles, suspension, etc.

vapour /ˈveɪpə(r)/ *n* [U15, T2] a gas that can be liquefied by increasing its pressure

vernier /ˈvɜːnɪə(r)/ *n* [U29, T2] a measuring gauge fitted with an auxiliary scale which allows the operator to read the main scale with an accuracy of one tenth of a division

waisting /ˈweɪstɪŋ/ *n* [U26, T7] deformation which brings about narrowing of the section of a rod or material under tension

wave power /ˈweɪv ˌpaʊə(r)/ *n* [U17, T9] a method of generating electricity by using the movement of waves in water

work volume /ˈwɜːk ˌvɒljuːm/ *n* [U28, T4] the space volume into which the manipulator of a robot can be positioned; hence the volume where useful work can be done

yaw /jɔː/ *n* [U28, T8] angular rotation about a vertical axis

yield point /ˈjiːld pɔɪnt/ *n* [U26, T7] the point where the elastic limit is reached